astro sex

what the stars say
about our sexuality

astro
sex

Amina Sutter ✳ Amal Tahir

illustrated by Anaïs Peyraud

STERLING ETHOS
New York

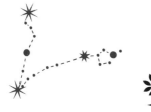

STERLING ETHOS
New York

French text © 2022 Amina Sutter and Amal Tahir
English translation © 2024 Sterling Publishing Co., Inc.

ISBN 978-1-4549-5081-3
ISBN 978-1-4549-5082-0 (e-book)

Library of Congress Control Number: 2023938589

For information about custom editions, special sales, and premium purchases, please contact specialsales@unionsquareandco.com.

Printed in India

2 4 6 8 10 9 7 5 3 1

unionsquareandco.com

Original cover design by Johanna Fritz, adapted by Stacy Wakefield Forte
Cover illustration by Anaïs Peyraud, © 2022 Fleurus Editions
Interior design by Johanna Fritz

Contents

Preface

AMINA AND AMAL. Taurus and Virgo. Two souls evolving, each walking their own path. And yet they manage to meet, totally by chance: one in Lisbon, the other in Brussels.

Despite the physical distance, their connection is incredibly powerful. Do you know how love at first sight feels? Well, that is exactly what our souls experienced. The first time we talked, everything was obvious, simple, as if our souls already knew each other.

It's true that we are both earth signs, but in reality, we share so much more than that. Amal is an Aquarius rising and approaches things in a unique way. Her brand is singularity. Amina is an Aries rising and approaches things with determination, grabbing every opportunity that crosses her path. Both of our Moon signs are Gemini. You can imagine that a lot of our video calls made no sense: we talked about everything and anything, and we could only be productive after having chatted about our lives for an hour first.

But what unites us the most is our desire to offer you, the reader, something different: a book mixing astrology and sexuality, which will allow you to go far beyond what you thought possible, and in which, thanks to the stars, you will learn to decipher both yours and your partner's sexual potential.

Amal

I really wanted to forge a tangible bond between my different hobbies: love and sexuality on one hand, and astrology on the other. I felt that these two worlds were connected, but I wanted to create a project with someone as convinced as me that there was a link between these two fields.

That's when I met Amina. I had bought myself a birth chart reading, and magic happened.

Amina is as passionate about astrology and sexuality as I am about eating burrata with cherry tomatoes. After many hours spent thinking and trying to understand this connection better, we decided to invite you into our world: deciphering your sexuality through the stars.

In this book, you will get to know me: I'm a perfectionist and a control freak, with a smidgen of eccentricity and Mars in Scorpio (a fact which you will understand later, if you don't already). This part of myself, as well as my Venus in Libra, led me toward a job investigating different matters of love and sexuality. When I became a neuroscience coach specializing in the fields of love and sexuality, I felt that I was truly combining my passions.

I live in Brussels, but I'm a worldly child. Like my Venus in Libra, I like to flutter around, and I quickly fall in love with a town, then another, and another . . .

I began my life path by studying to become a midwife, but it quickly stopped working for me: I needed more freedom, more depth.

Because I'm fascinated by human beings and how we function, I naturally turned to neuroscience coaching, spending a year learning and developing my skills. At the same time, I decided I should specialize in love and positive sexuality. I built my company during this time as well.

I also created an Instagram account, @amaltahir, which I use to share my thoughts about love, sex, money . . . Basically everything I love.

In my daily life, I coach women to help them connect to their inner goddess and reach orgasm. I also write books and host conferences. It's constant bliss. So now that we've gotten to know each other: *Welcome, baby!*

Astral ID

Rising: Aquarius

Sun: Virgo

Moon: Gemini

Mars: Scorpio

Venus: Libra

Is anyone really surprised that love and sexuality are at the center of my job?

Amina

Entrepreneur, professional astrologer, and creator of an astrology-focused Instagram account and brand, I'm not only passionate about astrology: it runs through my veins. I can't spend an hour without talking about it, and I unconsciously use every opportunity life offers to analyze it in the prism of astrology.

My mission is to help you rediscover yourself through the stars, so you can finally learn to fully accept and love yourself. As you will notice in these pages, I do so with a touch of humor, because with a Moon in Gemini, you must understand that fun is essential to me—just like the depth of my emotions and my spiritual connection are caused by my Mars (rising planet) in Pisces, in the twelfth House.

Astral ID

Rising: Aries

Sun: Taurus

Moon: Gemini

Mars: Pisces

Venus: Pisces

Is anyone really surprised that I love love?

Introduction

NOW THAT YOU KNOW a little bit more about us, you may be wondering why exactly we decided to write together, how we picked the guiding principles for this project, and in which mindset we birthed this powerful book.

Amina's Flashback

During our birth chart reading, I could sense that Amal was very excited, and that she had something to tell me. Always the good astrologer, I tried to stay as focused as I could, and I kept explaining to her my interpretation of her birth chart.

At the end of our interview, she expressed her gratitude to me, and described how she felt about my analysis. A big smile curved her lips, and she seamlessly told me that she wanted us to write a book together. I looked at her, wide-eyed, in awe of what she had just suggested.

She kept going: "Yes, I've been looking for an astrologer to write a book with me about sex and astrology for about a year. When I stumbled upon your Instagram account a few weeks ago, I immediately knew you were the one, and I booked this reading with you to better feel your energy and how you approach astrology."

It was crazy, because I knew the Universe had something in store for me: when Amal had booked the meeting, something quite magical happened.

Amal had managed to book a birth chart reading with me, even though I had closed my orders. It was thus impossible to book an appointment with me . . . When I received the email confirming Amal's order, I didn't understand what was happening.

And when I saw her name, I thought I had already seen it some-where. So, I ran to her Instagram and immediately understood that this wasn't going to be a simple birth chart reading. The Universe had a surprise for me . . .

So here I am, at the end of the interview, holding a gift from life in my hands. To be honest, I had never thought about writing a book before. I always thought it wasn't for me (and I was quite wrong about that!).

And yet, Amal's offer echoed with a big YES in me. Having a receptive and intuitive nature, I immediately accepted, laughing to myself while thinking about how my studies in literature were finally going to come in handy.

Is This Book Right for You?

This book is for all the people curious about astrology or sexuality. I would even say that it's simply made for all the people eager to discover new things.

To dive into this book, there is no prerequisite. Whether you're a novice in astrology, or a confirmed astrology aficionado, we hope you will find something to quench your curiosity and nourish your knowledge about yourself and others. The keyword for us here is *fulfillment*.

A Little Clarification Before
Diving into the Stars

Before we can let you immerse yourself in our book, we would like to clarify a few points.

Astrology is a vast and complex world. This book obviously cannot address all the subtleties of this practice. If you wish to go further, don't hesitate to read other books with a more general approach to astrology, or that talk about how astrology can be applied to everyday life issues. Astrology is an endless subject, with infinite ramifications. We could talk about it for days, even years. There is always something to say, analyze, and interpret.

This is why it was essential for us in this book to clearly define what we wanted to talk about. And considering the things we were both interested in, we chose to focus first and foremost on love and sex. This book also cannot fully analyze your personal birth chart. For that, you need to go see an astrologer, for there are so many nuances that every birth chart is unique. And more importantly, don't take everything at face value, because the format forces us to make generalizations. Our goal is that this book will make you want to anchor yourself in your astral chart, so you can draw on its resources.

Furthermore, if you feel like astrology is your life path, and you dream of becoming an astrologer, Amina's Instagram account is full of information, and she herself is a tutor.

The Itinerary of Our
Astral Journey

Now that we have cleared that up, let's discover the different steps of our journey.

The first part of this book will give you an introduction to astrology, in which Amina will explain the basics, including astrological signs' descriptions, obviously, but also plenty of other essential information that will help you understand your birth chart.

In the second part, Amal will cover the basics of love and sexuality, because what interests us here is not only that you discover what lies behind your birth chart, but that you also learn things about love and sexuality.

In the third part, Amina will analyze sexuality through the lens of astrology. Thanks to this section, you will know which astrological placements in your birth chart can help you understand your relationship to love and sexuality.

Finally, in the fourth part, Amal will explain which sex toys you can use according to your astrological sign.

Isn't this a magical program? To fully absorb it, we advise you to keep a little "astro notebook" next to you while you read. You can use it to take notes and do the exercises we've slipped into the book.

We both have our Moon in Gemini, so we both love to have fun. Thus, this book will be punctuated with little jokes and anecdotes about the placements, the sole purpose of which is to make astrology seem less austere and to make you laugh, and maybe make your friends laugh, too, if you share some of this at parties.

The organization of this book is designed to allow you to read it in the way that best suits you. You can see it as a journey, taking you from one thing to the next, or you can pick a section according to your whims. While hanging out with friends, for example, you can go directly to the "astrological compatibilities" section to help the people you're with know themselves better.

Finally, we wanted to specify that we will use the terms "feminine energy" and "masculine energy" throughout this book. However,

they absolutely aren't references to gender, but rather to spiritual concepts from the yin and the yang.

Since this book is written by two feminists of color, we obviously want it to be as inclusive as possible (which is normal in this day and age, right?). That is why whenever we talk about relationships and love, we extend beyond the confines of heteronormativity: you can love whomever you want.

And now we wish you a good reading, beautiful soul.

Amina & Amal

1

at the heart of astrology

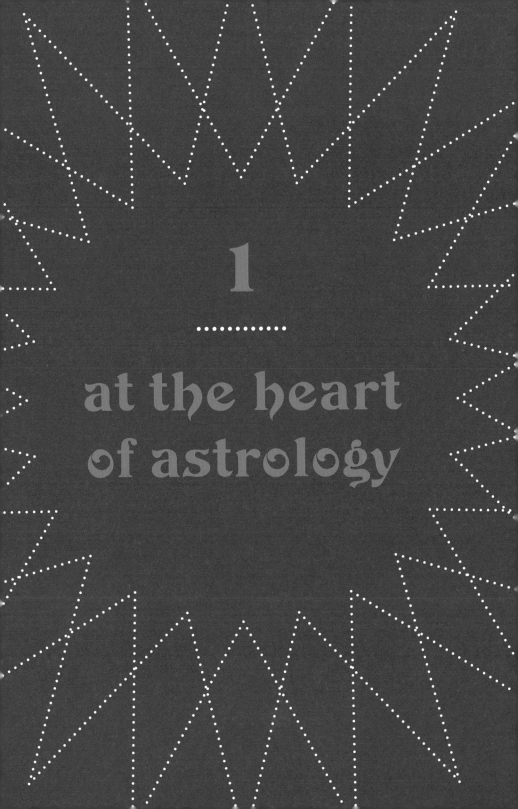

Astrology as a Tool for Self-Fulfillment

—— "What is astrology, actually?" ——

It's a question you may have already asked yourself while taking your bath, in bed before sleep, or while you were running on a treadmill at the gym.

Astrology is a discipline that has existed since the dawn of time and that, despite centuries of glory, was largely criticized after the nineteenth century. And yet, a new evolution is happening nowadays, with our perception of astrology shifting from an amused reading of the morning horoscope in the newspaper toward its more popular current status as a tool for self-development and self-love.

In the past several years, we have noticed that astrology seems to be resonating with more and more people: Instagram is full of accounts sharing info about astrology, and in libraries, the accordant sections get bigger every year. It shows that in our current society, people are interested in this field.

Think about yourself: maybe you know your loved ones' zodiac signs, even though you didn't seem to care about it before? Maybe you've even tried to know more about your crush by using astrology? As you can see, using astrology is getting more and more mainstream, and I must say I'm very excited about it.

Of course, and like in every field, it's important to pick your sources with care. By the way, stay safe: birth charts are actually quite intimate, so watch who you share yours with. Promise?

"What exactly is it for?"

Nowadays we mostly use astrology to learn more about our personality. There are many ways to employ this extraordinary tool. It's very useful to find out our strengths and potential, or when we want to learn more about our soul wounds. And this is true of every field, whether it's your passions, your life path, or your professional life. The possibilities are endless!

"What is your background?"

I personally discovered astrology by chance, during a trip to London. I passed by a book whose black cover caught my eye in a bookstore window. I didn't understand what had happened in me, and I didn't buy it . . . It was only when I got back to the apartment I was renting that I started to regret this decision, and thoughts of that book then haunted me all night.

The next day, I returned to the store to buy it. That's when I felt struck by lightning. You could say I literally became obsessed with astrology in less than twenty-four hours.

I quickly went into the subject in depth, and after six months of self-taught and intense exploration, I decided to get professional training. Today I am a passionate astrologer, and I wish to offer you the chance to learn how to use this tool to truly meet yourself and feel love for yourself, your life, and your own magic.

"Isn't it too complicated to understand?"

It's true that this is a complicated field. And yet, its definition is rather simple: astrology is a system that aims to study and explain the correlation between planetary movements and how they influence events on earth, both on an individual and a collective level.

Astrology is much more than what you read in horoscopes, or what you can see in funny Instagram memes. It's a hypercomplex system, and its purpose is to give you a map—which means a sort of user's manual—that you can use to know what your soul is looking for on Earth. Thanks to this map, you can understand who you are, what your potential and strengths are, but also what sensitive areas you need to work on in this life.

This discipline can help you shine a new light on yourself, and help you accept and love yourself deeply. It can also make it easier for you to understand the people around you: who they are, how they work, and much more.

Astrology allows us to step away from a self-centered point of view, and to understand that each person is unique and wonderful, both in light and darkness.

I also want to say that if you ever see online content in social media calling a zodiac sign "toxic" or "bad," know that it's completely false. In astrology, there's no such thing as a bad placement: nothing is negative. Every aspect of your chart represents a chance to grow, evolve, transcend.

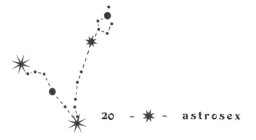

"So how does it work?"

In astrology, each planet, sign, astrological House, and aspect carries a meaning. To give you one example, your Venus placement will give you information about your relationship to love and your emotional needs. These meanings were established thousands of years ago, by knowledgeable people who studied the relations between planets' movements and the events on Earth.

Like I've said before, astrology is a complicated field. It can, however, be explained with the principles of quantum physics, which considers that everything is energy: our world is energy, we are energy, water is energy, the Earth and all that surrounds it is also energy.

Each planet has its own vibration, a particular frequency that influences us in a specific way. You also vibrate every minute of every day. And I would like to make you vibrate through my words, to help you discover the tool of astrology so you can easily and fully swim within yourself.

By the way, you may have felt the calling of this book's energy yourself, and it's not a coincidence! It's more proof that everything is energy.

Whether you are a novice, a connoisseur, or have experimented with astrology, Amal and I will take you by the hand to help you discover the depths of yourself and others through the stars.

We invite you to explore sexuality through the lens of astrology so you can learn to use it to understand and develop your sexual potential.

Discover Your Birth Chart

YOUR BIRTH CHART is simply the photograph of how the planets were arranged at your birth. This diagram shows us your Sun sign (which you probably already know), but also your other astrological placements: your rising sign, your Moon sign, your Mars sign, your Venus sign, and the one for all the other planets, and thus how they were placed in the Universe at the exact moment of your birth. Indeed, the day, month, and year of your birth (which determine your Sun sign) only give you a piece of all the information you need to generate your birth chart. Your time and place of birth will make it vibrate fully.

If you're into astrology, I'm sure your birth chart (also called natal chart) is already screenshotted on your phone, even in your favorite folder. However, if this is your first deep dive into this world, the first step is to create your birth chart.

Create Your Birth Chart

To get your natal chart, you will need the date, place, and time of your birth (make sure the time is precise). Once you have this information, visit a specialized website like astro.com. You then simply need to enter your info, click "continue," and the website will make all the complicated calculations for you, to generate your birth chart in a few seconds only. And that's it!

Some websites and apps will give you your info in a table, without the zodiac wheel. If you're really interested in astrology, I would advise you to familiarize yourself with the circular birth chart. I know it seems complicated to see everything and understand how it works at first. But trust my experience, you'll get it very quickly.

Furthermore, as an astrologer, I'm quite aware of how lucky we are to be able to get a birth chart so quickly and easily, with just a few clicks on a phone or a computer. Before the twenty-first century, the practice of astrology was reserved for a minority of people (mostly men). And even in the last century, before the invention of computers, it was very complicated to make the calculations that allowed us to create a natal chart. It requires hundreds of calculations and is an extremely long process to do ourselves.

So, you can understand why I won't explain here how to create your birth chart yourself, and why I am so grateful when I see that we can now discover ourselves through the stars after just a couple of clicks. By the way, if you're reading this book during a party with friends, don't hesitate to grab your phone to check out your birth chart!

To show you what a birth chart looks like, I generated one at random and recreated it on the next page. This is not one of our birth charts, because as an astrologer, I am aware that a birth chart is confidential and intimate. So, as I've said before, watch who you show yours to!

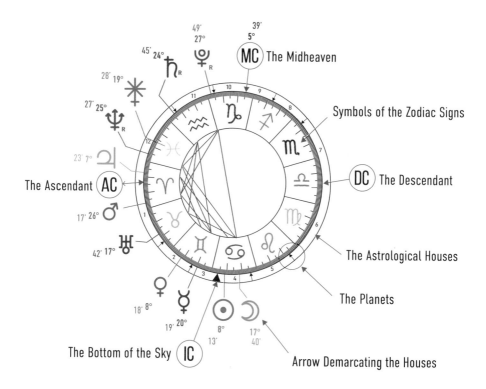

In the zodiac wheel, each of the twelve signs is represented by its symbol. They are always organized in order, starting with Aries and ending with Pisces.

The colored symbols outside of the wheel represent the planets of the solar system that we use in modern astrology, as well as the Sun, the Moon, and the asteroid Juno.

☉ Sun	♃ Jupiter
☽ Moon	♄ Saturn
☿ Mercury	♅ Uranus
♀ Venus	♆ Neptune
♂ Mars	♇ Pluto
	⚹ Juno

As for the angles, you can see the ascendant (also called the rising sign), which is symbolized by the letters AC (here, on the left). Also opposite, the letters DC show the descendant. At the top, you can see the Midheaven, symbolized by the letters MC, and finally, always opposite the Midheaven, you find the Bottom of the Sky.

On the outside circle of the wheel, you can see the twelve astrological Houses, demarcated by little arrows.

Thanks to this illustration, you can see that each planet is situated both in a sign and a House. Here, for instance, Venus is in the sign Gemini and in the second House, while the Sun and Moon are in the sign Cancer and the fourth House.

It's your turn now: create your birth chart and let's go!

Time to Jump!

That's it, you have your birth chart. Impressive, I know. The first time, we always wonder if we're going to be able to decipher this image, and if we will ever get used to its structure. Don't worry, you will quickly understand how it's built.

As I've said before, your birth chart is like a photograph of the planets' placement in the sky at the exact moment you took your first breath on Earth. Thus, it gives you a lot of information. Know that you could spend a lifetime trying to interpret it, that's how complex and multidimensional it is.

Each placement contains an infinity of possible interpretations that will all manifest in your life according to your experiences and the choices you'll make. Because if the planetary movements influence what happens on Earth, nothing is set in stone; on the contrary, no matter your birth chart, you have free will and nothing in astrology can dictate your behavior.

And by the way, interpreting a birth chart is an art. That's why different astrologers will read the same birth chart differently. Of course, the essence will remain the same, but it's true that there are as many birth chart interpretations as there are astrologers. This is what makes this profession so beautiful in my opinion.

I personally love when other astrologers analyze my birth chart. Even if I must admit that I know it by heart, I don't always have enough perspective on my own life to notice some things and understand them deeply. Indeed, we always receive messages right when we are ready to hear them. And since we are always growing and evolving, we constantly pick up on new things. Besides, I must say it's always a fascinating conversation.

☾ How to Read Your Birth Chart

Let's get back to your birth chart. As I've explained earlier, the different colored symbols on your zodiac wheel are the planets of the solar system as well as the Sun and Moon. Indeed, in astrology we treat the Luminaries as planets.

These planets are situated in signs, for each planet was at a specific place the moment you were born, and this place corresponds to a given sign to a degree. So, you may be a Taurus Sun, but also a Pisces Moon, a Geminin Venus, a Cancer Mars . . .

Then, you'll notice that planets placed in signs are also in Houses. The Houses represent the different aspects of life and are here to give us extra information to analyze the planet in each sign.

Finally, planets are connected to each other thanks to the red and blue lines that you can see on your birth chart. They are called the "aspects" and allow us to add nuance to the interpretation and can even totally alter the nature of a placement.

☾ The Luminaries

The Sun-Moon Duo

Together, the Sun and the Moon are an inseparable couple: they are the Luminaries. One emits light, the other reflects light. The Sun represents a "masculine" energy, or yang, while the Moon represents a "feminine" energy, or yin. We are here talking about the feminine and masculine energies as defined by the yin and the yang. These concepts have nothing to do with someone's sex or gender. These two energies exist and evolve within every living being.

The yang energy is called "masculine" because it pushes us to act and move forward, while the yin energy is called "feminine" because it invites us to welcome things in, to feel, and to be nourishing.

If the Sun pushes us to act, the Moon pushes us to react.

None of these energies is better than the other, they simply complement each other. The concepts of "feminine" and "masculine" energies are essential in this book, because they play a big part in the subject of sexuality.

 The Sun Sign

By now, you understand that you are much more than your Sun sign. I know it's very trendy lately to say that, but the trust is that it's a really important nuance. Because whenever you say that you're a Taurus or a Scorpio, you're only talking about which zodiac sign the Sun was placed on at the time of your birth.

Even so, the Sun plays an important role in your birth chart: in astrology it is seen as the center of the Universe and as a result, the center of all the things in your birth chart. Without this placement, nothing would make sense.

The Sun represents your Self in its purest form: your essence and your inner radiance. Your purpose is (among other things) to become this inner radiance. By connecting to the energy of your Sun sign, you will learn to love yourself, and to be confident about who you truly are.

 The Moon Sign

Natural satellite of the Earth, the Moon is just as important as the Sun.

Your Moon sign represents your inner Self, the most hidden and even mysterious part of yourself. It's the sign that indicates how you react in your everyday life, what your emotional needs are, how you take care of others, and how others should take care of *you*.

The Moon sign is harder to analyze than the Sun sign. Unlike the latter, which represents the most conscious part of ourselves, the Moon sign touches the unconscious of someone. Its energy is cyclical, fluid, and receptive. It invites us to connect to the flow and the changing nature of our inner life.

☾ The Personal Planets

The planets called "personal" give us information about your personality. They include the Luminaries we just talked about, as well as Mercury, Venus, and Mars.

Mercury

Mercury is the smallest planet in our solar system, and the closest to the Sun. It's also the fastest, for it completes its revolution around the Sun in only eighty-eight days.

In astrology, Mercury represents intellect, communication, and everything that goes through our head. That includes how you think, talk, or write; your memory; and the way you share information.

It will indicate, for example, if you're eloquent or not, if you're direct and talk without thinking, or if, on the contrary, you struggle to find the right words to express how you feel. It can even reveal whether you have the potential to have a melodious voice.

It's also the planet that will inform you on how you think: Is your thoughts pattern linear or in a tree structure?

Mercury's energy is fast, and mostly multidirectional. It pushes you to bond, but also to show curiosity and analyze details.

Finally, Mercury is the planet of learning, and it is also about technology and short-distance travels.

Venus

Venus has a "feminine" and passive energy. It's the planet that represents how we spread our love, giving you precious indications on how you love, your love language, how you walk into a new relationship, your emotional needs, and everything you love in general.

It also explains your relationship to beauty and harmony, and its energy invites you to add beauty in your life.

Because of its yin polarity, Venus is a planet that allows us to receive. Thus, it represents our ability to be receptive when it comes to financial abundance, but not only.

 Mars

On the contrary, Mars is a "masculine" energy, and is thus active, direct, and penetrative, and questions the notion of combativeness. It shows how you use the energy of your Sun sign.

Mars is the impulse of life, the principle of action, bravery, and boldness; it's how you undertake things and act. The red planet needs a mission; it needs to be in motion. It also symbolizes passion, the spark of life, and your sexual needs.

In this book, we will talk in detail about Venus and Mars, since they are the most important planets, the planets that animate affection and sexual energy. You will learn more about this in the third part of the book, because when talking about sex and astrology, it's more relevant to analyze the Mars placement than, for example, the Sun placement.

☾ The Social and Generational Planets

I will dwell less on these other planets, for they don't express as many things about who you are and your personality, while this is really the core of the book.

The Social Planets

The social planets talk about our relationship with the collective. They are Jupiter and Saturn.

Jupiter is the principle of expansion, abundance, luck, and social accomplishments. It helps us dream big and have faith our luck will hold.

Saturn is the principle of structure, seriousness, and discipline. This planet helps us be more disciplined, manifest seriousness and maturity, and build solid foundations and patience. It can also represent the challenges of life, meant to help us grow and evolve.

The Generational Planets

Uranus, Neptune, and Pluto are the generational planets.

Uranus is the principle of invention and revolution, change, and radical rupture.

Neptune is the principle of intuitive inspiration, universality, and spirituality.

And Pluto is the principle of transformation, regeneration, and divine destruction.

☾ The Zodiac Signs

The twelve zodiac signs, of which you see the symbols all around the wheel, are archetypes. Their pure energy helps us interpret the placements (for example, Venus in Cancer). By understanding the energies of the twelve zodiac signs, you will find it easier to decipher your birth chart on your own, without having to read the placement's description every time. This is how I teach the students learning birth chart readings with me.

Each sign carries an element and a modality. There are four elements (fire, earth, air, and water) and three modalities (cardinal, fixed, and mutable). Each sign from the same element has a different modality and vice versa. That's why each sign is unique. For example, among the fire signs, Aries has a cardinal modality, Leo has a fixed modality, and Sagittarius has a mutable modality. This is what gives them very different characteristics, even if they're united by the same element.

And so, there are different ways to divide the zodiac, such as:

- in four, with the elements;
- in three, with the modalities.

You may ask yourself what the elements represent, and you might have never heard of the word *modality*. Come with me, I will explain this all to you quite simply.

The Elements

In astrology, elements represent both an energy and a way to approach life. Signs with the same element share some qualities, so even if they're very different they have a common ground.

Fire signs: Aries, Leo, and Sagittarius

Shared characteristics: passion, energy, positivity, instinct, spontaneity, and motivation

> **amal's fun fact** I am a Virgo, and I could never get along with fire signs: they were too . . . fiery for me. But during my spiritual awakening, I connected to my freedom, my spontaneity, and my passion, and I quickly attracted various fire signs. That's when I realized that the issue wasn't that I didn't like fire signs, but that I didn't like my fire side. Once I reconciled with this side of myself, I was able to evolve.

Earth signs: Taurus, Virgo, and Capricorn

Shared characteristics: pragmatism, grounding, practicality, stability, honesty, reliability, and patience

Air signs: Gemini, Libra, and Aquarius
Shared characteristics: curiosity, sociability, communication, learning, casualness, and logic

Water signs: Cancer, Scorpio, and Pisces
Shared characteristics: sensitivity, intuition, creativity, inner spirituality, and empathy

The Modalities

In astrology, modalities are yet other indicators and bring nuance. Signs with the same modality have a few shared characteristics and a common ground.

Cardinal signs: Aries, Cancer, Libra, and Capricorn.
They are here to begin each of the four seasons.
Shared characteristics: They are leaders, they love to create and take actions, and they are good at undertaking things.

Fixed signs: Taurus, Leo, Scorpio, and Aquarius.
They are here to ground a season.
Shared characteristics: stability, grounding, endurance, perseverance; they like to give a sense of security and can be stubborn.

Mutable signs: Gemini, Virgo, Sagittarius, and Pisces.
They are here to end a season.
Shared characteristics: innovation, adaptability, open-mindedness; they are always moving and have a fluid energy.

The Axes

There is a very important last thing to understand when talking about zodiac signs.

In astrology, everything works according to the axes, as you can see on the birth chart on page 24. Each sign has an opposite sign that completes it. The opposite sign is everything the other sign is not and possesses all its complementary qualities. Here are the opposite signs:

- Aries is Libra's opposite.
- Taurus is Scorpio's opposite.
- Gemini is Sagittarius's opposite.
- Cancer is Capricorn's opposite.
- Leo is Aquarius's opposite.
- Virgo is Pisces's opposite.

You may wonder if opposite signs are too different to get along. They aren't, and actually we can often feel attraction for the opposite energy, whether it's your zodiac sign's opposite, your rising sign's opposite, or even any other zodiac sign that predominates your birth chart.

☾ Angles, Houses, and Ruling Planets

The Angles

The Ascendant: The Star of Angles

Your ascendant sign, or rising sign, is the one that rose on the horizon on the moment of your birth. In your birth chart, it is accompanied by the letters AC.

The ascendant is not a celestial body, but an angle. This angle plays a crucial part. Some astrologers even believe the rising sign to be more important than the Sun sign. Because beyond its meaning in your natal chart, which is very indicative of how you introduce yourself to others, it's also the sign that will give rhythm to your birth chart.

Your rising sign thus represents the unique way with which you enter the world. It's the mask you wear every day, the first thing people will see when they meet you. For instance, if you are a Pisces with a Leo rising, your true essence—meaning who you are inside—is connected to the Pisces archetype, but the way you are perceived is influenced by the Leo sign.

You can now better understand why when someone you don't know asks you to guess their zodiac sign, you are unlikely to succeed. In fact, you can only see their mask just like they can only see yours. So, instead of asking people to guess your Sun sign at parties, ask them to guess your rising sign! You'll see, it's more fun.

amal and amina's fun fact Once, I was literally crying while waiting for my inscription for a clinical sexologist university course to be validated, but on the phone the lady had explained to me that my case was "particular" and the team needed more time to make a decision.

In tears, I sent audio messages to Amina on WhatsApp. Amina replied: "Amal, you are an Aquarius rising. Everything you do, you will do it differently. But if you make peace with this part of yourself, you will feel better."

I cried even more, because ever since I was a kid, I could always feel I had a different way to approach people, things, life. And thanks to Amina, I finally made peace with this side of my personality, and I understood it was in fact a strength.

This is a little anecdote to show you again that astrology is really a tool for self-development, and that's pretty amazing!

The Descendant, the Bottom of the Sky, and the Midheaven

The ascendant is not the only angle that astrology takes into consideration.

Facing the ascendant, there is another angle: **the descendant** (DC). The descendant represents the other part of us that we will attract into our relationships. We can see it as the mirror effect of our life, meaning the part of us we tend to reject.

If you meet someone with a Sun or rising sign identical to your descendant sign, you might be annoyed by some of their characteristics, and might even find it hard to stand them. It's normal. However, I invite you to question yourself: Is this a characteristic that is part of me and that I struggle to accept?

If you know your rising sign, discover your descendant sign, facing it in the table below:

Aries	Libra
Taurus	Scorpio
Gemini	Sagittarius
Cancer	Capricorn
Leo	Aquarius
Virgo	Pisces

At the bottom of the birth chart, there is the **Bottom of the Sky** (IC on the chart, because it is also called *Imum Coeli* in astrology). This angle represents our roots, our ancestral lineage, the home we grew up in, and more generally, our interiority.

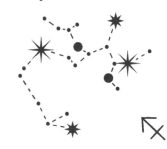

Finally, the highest point of the map is the **Midheaven** (MC). It represents our social status, our reputation, and our career over the course of our life.

The Houses

If the rising sign is here to give rhythm to the birth chart, it's because it defines the position of the planets in their respective Houses, which allows us to refine the interpretation of your chart.

Like with zodiac signs, there are twelve Houses. Each House represents different aspects of life. I will tell you more about Houses once we have covered the different energies of the zodiac signs. But before I can do that, there's one last important notion I need to explain.

The Ruling Planets

As we have seen already, each sign has an element and a modality, and it also possesses an opposite sign that completes it. Well, each sign is also ruled by a planet, and this planet will give it all of its energetic vibration.

So, whenever you read in books or Instagram posts the "ruling of X sign," it means the ruling planet of this sign. The Sun, for example, is the ruling planet of Leo.

Here is a little table to recap the ruling planets:

Planets	Signs
Sun	Leo
Moon	Cancer
Mercury	Gemini and Virgo
Venus	Taurus and Libra
Mars	Aries and Scorpio*
Jupiter	Sagittarius and Pisces*
Saturn	Capricorn and Aquarius*
Uranus	Aquarius
Neptune	Pisces
Pluto	Scorpio

*These signs have two ruling planets: a traditional ruling planet and a modern ruling planet. The traditional ruling planet is simply the planet astrologers used to pair in ancient astrology, before the discovery of Uranus (1781), Neptune (1846), and Pluto (1930). Scorpio was then ruled by Mars, Aquarius by Saturn, and Pisces by Jupiter.

amina's note I know that a lot of modern astrologers no longer use the traditional ruling planets, but I personally still use them (as well as the modern ruling planets) in my practice of astrology. Indeed, even if they were discovered earlier, these three planets only became ruling planets much later. This is because between the Renaissance and the twentieth century, the historical and scientific changes caused a decline of astrology in the West. I also personally resonate a lot with their associations to the relevant signs.

The Energies of the Zodiac Signs

AND NOW, let me take you on a tour of the placements through the twelve zodiac signs, to better help you understand the energies. Along the way, you will find information about your ascendant, your Sun sign, and your Moon sign. Have a nice trip!

Aries

A cardinal fire sign, ruled by the planet Mars.

The Aries is the trailblazer of the zodiac. Since it's the first sign, it's also the spark that can light up the fire and give the first impulse to the zodiac wheel.

The Aries is passionate, hot-headed, and instinctive. As a cardinal fire sign, Aries act in a direct and impulsive way; they cannot wait because they are pushed by their desire to begin and fight. They need to move and move on, whatever happens. It's also due to the energy granted to them by the planet Mars.

Aries's bravery stems from their naivety: because Aries is the first sign, they don't know what comes before them and are inexperienced.

With a self-absorbed nature, the Aries know how to assert themselves and place boundaries skillfully. They don't beat around the bush and can lack subtlety.

ARIES RISING

With an Aries rising, you are basking in energy and vitality, and you give off the image of a self-confident person.

You have a strong connection to your yang energy, and with you, things need to move: you like when things move fast and you have a pretty impatient nature.

At first glance, you thus look like a dynamic, passionate, and vivacious person, and you also struggle to hide how you feel: when you're happy, it shows, and when you're less happy . . . it also shows.

ARIES SUN

You show initiative and you know how to be brave. You're also an enthusiastic, hot-headed, and passionate person who doesn't waste their time.

With an enterprising spirit, you know how to assert yourself and hate being told what to do.

Your connection to your inner fire is deep, and you need to learn to channel your energy. Otherwise, you might see it turn into fits of anger.

ARIES MOON

With this placement, you can be very vivacious and impulsive emotionally, because you feel your emotions very strongly. They are always boiling, and when they overflow, they can explode. So, make sure your words or actions don't go beyond what you mean.

It's essential for you to live and deal with what you feel. The good thing is that you're an uncompromising, honest, and genuine person.

Taurus

Fixed earth sign, ruled by the planet Venus.

Taurus is a sign of concretization and materialization.

With the Taurus, things are grounded and stable. Connected to their body and constantly looking for pleasure and enjoyment, they exist in the world using their five senses: touch, sight, taste, hearing, and smell. These senses are some of the first motivations of this sign.

The Taurus energy is soft and calm, and they feel a deep need for things to be slow. They can, however, be very stubborn, and they can struggle to step out of their comfort zone.

Connected to the energy of Venus, the Taurus has good taste and enjoys beautiful things, like art, fashion, and interior design.

TAURUS RISING

You have a stable energy, and endurance is one of your strong suits. You have a strong body, and the ability to substantially improve your physical strength.

You give off the image of a stable and charming person, with a sense of style, and one who can look on the bright side.

The search for pleasure and sensory experiences are two essential motivations for you.

TAURUS SUN

You have a persevering, calm, and stable nature.

You are defined by your sensuality and your charm, and you like to enjoy the pleasures of life, taking your time to savor each moment.

When you want something, you don't easily give up and you can even be stubborn.

Change can be hard for you, which explains why you prefer comfort over adventures.

TAURUS MOON

With a motherly nature, you know how to take care of the people you love, but you also have a deep need for safety to be emotionally stable. You can also be very attached to your materialistic possessions.

With this placement, you have a strong need for slowness and gentleness in your life.

Gemini

Mutable air sign, ruled by the planet Mercury.

With the Gemini we are carried by a soft and refreshing breath of air: the Gemini energy is light, fun, and flexible.

The Gemini is curious and naturally very connected to their intellect. This sign is quick and loves to both learn many things and teach these things to everyone around them.

They have kept their childlike innocence, and the energy of an eternal teenager, which makes Gemini a mischievous sign who loves to play.

Sociable, the Gemini is also very good with words, and can be an unmatched orator or a great author.

GEMINI RISING

Your energy is overflowing, and you can go in all the directions at once.

You have a gift for building relationships, so you may seem very sociable.

Whenever you meet someone, you are motivated by novelty and intellectual stimulation.

With this placement, you may seem younger than you are.

GEMINI SUN

With a flexible and curious nature, no one is ever bored around you. You also love to share and teach your knowledge.

You love to start a lot of things at once, but you don't often go in depth with them, and you may struggle to finish what you have started.

You are a fun and laid-back person. You like to make sure life is casual, and you're easygoing.

GEMINI MOON

You need things in life to be fun and casual so you can blossom and feel in accordance with yourself.

With this placement, you can have a great need to communicate even though you may scatter yourself when trying to express yourself.

Emotionally speaking, things are not always easy for you, and you may tend to intellectualize your emotions instead of just feeling them.

Cancer

Cardinal water sign, ruled by the Moon.

Immersed in their inner world, the Cancer is very sensitive and navigates the world through their feelings. Their energy is soft, calm, and tranquil.

Because they feel everything strongly, the Cancer tends to protect themselves a lot. At first glance, they can seem reserved, even wary, but once you earn their trust, the Cancer opens up and gives a lot.

Hugs, little attentions, affectionate gestures of all kinds . . . The Cancer likes to take care of others, to nourish and mother others. Ruled by the Moon, this water sign is very creative and has an over-flowing imagination. They also love to daydream, warm and safe in the home they built with love and care.

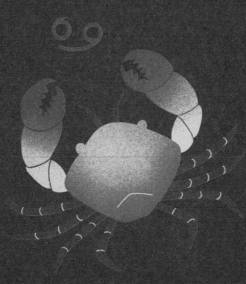

CANCER RISING

You seem to be a soft and deeply kind person.

You get in touch with the world through feelings, and you are very sensitive to your environment's energy.

However, be careful not to absorb other people's energy too much. It could pile up in you and make you stagnate.

CANCER SUN

You have a soft, thoughtful, and tender nature. With you, people feel wrapped up in love.

When you meet someone new, you can be wary and struggle to open up. But once you let people into your universe, you are fully involved in the relationship.

You are also sensitive and at times, you can have your head in the clouds.

CANCER MOON

You are very sensitive, and you feel your emotions strongly. It is thus important for you to understand your emotional nature, so you can deal with your feelings and learn to better live with them.

With this placement, you may have a very developed maternal instinct, and you like to take care of your loved ones.

However, be careful not to be too touchy, and not to take things to heart too much.

Leo

Fixed fire sign, ruled by the Sun.

The Leo is here to shine, spread their light all around them, and invite the world to shine too. The Leo invites people to dare to be fully themselves, and to be confident in who they are. The Leo energy is tender, warm, and positive.

It's an extroverted sign, to whom other people's opinions are quite important. As a fixed sign, the Leo knows how to be loyal and persevering, but also a little bit stubborn.

The Leo is an uncompromising sign who doesn't do things halfway, kind of like the Sagittarius. With the Leo, it's all or nothing, and because they're romantic, this can lead them to express their love in a spectacular and extraordinary way.

LEO RISING

When you walk into a room, people immediately notice you. You shine with your presence and your tangible warm energy.

Even if you struggle to admit it, you can sometimes look for other people's approval before you undertake to do something.

LEO SUN

Leader with a big heart and a childlike soul, you are a joyous, positive, and most importantly a generous person.

With a Sun in Leo, you are a very loyal person.

You know how to brilliantly motivate and lead the people around you, which allows you to give them a boost.

You can still be a bit too self-centered and focused on your own needs at times.

LEO MOON

You need to feel seen and heard, and for the focus to be on you.

As a romantic person, you have a big heart and when you love someone, you love deeply. You know how to show your love with spectacular and extraordinary gestures.

You can be a bit of a "drama queen" sometimes; you live your emotions deeply and sometimes in a theatrical way. However, be careful not to exaggerate how you feel just to be the center of attention.

Virgo

Mutable earth sign, ruled by Mercury.

Purity, helpfulness, and organization: these are the keywords of the Virgo.

It's a sign who is oriented toward others, a sign of self-sacrifice who can sometimes think about themselves last, putting others before them.

As far as organization goes, the Virgo is efficient and straight-forward. They know how they want things to be done, which can sometimes lead them to be overly controlling. They can be too demanding and a bit of a perfectionist. This is probably why it's a hardworking sign, who loves hard work, too.

Ruled by Mercury, the Virgo is also good at analyzing and observing: no details get past them.

VIRGO RISING

With a rising in Virgo, you watch the world with an analytical eye. You notice everything around you: it's as if you existed in the world with magnifying glasses, allowing you to observe every detail.

At first glance you are a reserved person, because you like knowing who you're dealing with before you get involved in a relationship.

VIRGO SUN

You are a hardworking and efficient person, but you know how to stay humble: you don't necessarily need outside validation. In fact, your inner critic (who is very demanding) is often the one telling you whether you are happy with your accomplishments.

You are big-hearted, loyal, and helpful. People can rely on you no matter what.

One of your superpowers is your ability to organize everything methodically and pragmatically. Plus, as we all know, you love it. But be careful not to bother your Pisces friends too much; they don't possess the same organizational qualities.

VIRGO MOON

You have a deeply analytical side, and because you hate mess, it reassures you to feel like you've got everything under control.

You struggle to take your feelings into consideration because you intellectualize them too much.

You are often overly critical of yourself. Be careful about that, because with this placement, you can become too strict with yourself. I'm thus inviting you to be kinder to yourself.

Libra

Cardinal air sign, ruled by Venus.

As the relational sign par excellence, the Libra is the diplomat of the zodiac. It's a sign oriented toward others, who prioritizes peace and harmony above all. The Libra naturally abhors conflict and knows how to ensure that people around them get along.

Ruled by Venus, this air sign enters relationships and easily shares with others with charm and beauty.

Just like the Taurus, the Libra is naturally good at everything linked to Venus's energy, whether it be decoration, fashion, or art in general.

LIBRA RISING

You are perceived as a sociable and charming person, because you enter new relationships with ease, and you explore the world while paying attention to the beauty all around.

You naturally care about social well-being. You are also able to see and understand all points of view, and you know how to be very empathetic.

LIBRA SUN

You learn to know yourself and who you are through others, like a mirror effect. That is why relationships are so important in your life.

You are animated by a strong sense of justice: you love for things to be fair, and you know how to hear and understand all points of view.

You have taste and an eye for art, which allows you to bring beauty all around you.

LIBRA MOON

Harmony and balance are essential to your emotional well-being, and you tend to keep your emotions to yourself in fear of creating conflicts.

With this placement, you can be a very imaginative person who loves to create beautiful things. During difficult times, you can find refuge in your artistic creation, whatever the medium is.

Scorpio

Fixed water sign, ruled by the planets Mars and Pluto.

Mysterious and hard to grasp, the Scorpio is a sign of great personal power and intensity.

Very connected to the depth of their own soul and their darkest side, they know how to dig deep to see what is really happening within them to radically transform themselves. Like the Phoenix, they know how to destroy everything so they can be reborn from their ashes and evolve on their own path.

Fascinated by human psychology, they also love to deeply understand others. With them, it's all or nothing, and they hate superficiality.

With a deep need to preserve their intimacy, the Scorpio knows how to sort out their relationships, and would rather stay alone or with people they really trust, and with whom they feel safe.

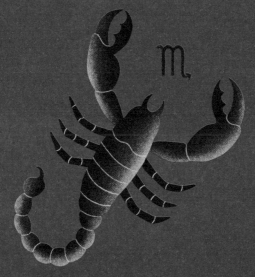

SCORPIO RISING

You are perceived as a secretive and mysterious person.

You feel the energies of all the things around you. You often show great intuition, and your instinct is never wrong.

The magnetic aura you emit can be very attractive.

SCORPIO SUN

You are on this Earth to live intense and deep transformations, which perhaps explains your attraction to everything mystical, intangible, and taboo, including regarding sexuality.

Because you have very developed critical thinking and detail-oriented observational skills, nothing gets past you.

Your intuition is quite developed, and your instincts are never wrong. So you should learn to listen to yourself, since it is one of your greatest superpowers.

SCORPIO MOON

With this placement, you can't just stick to appearances, and you hate superficiality. You love to dig deep above all else.

Perpetually questioning the meaning of your life, crisis and self-reassessment are part of your everyday life.

Furthermore, you feel your emotions strongly and intensely, but you need great trust to live these emotions around other people.

Sagittarius

Mutable fire sign, ruled by Jupiter.

    The Sagittarius invites us to expand: ourselves, our beliefs, our ideas, and our dreams. It's a deeply human and joyous sign, open to enthusiasm and adventure.

    Ruled by the planet Jupiter, this sign has great insight: they aim always higher with their arrow, so they can dream big, and they never fear to step out of their comfort zone to chase their craziest dream, go further, and surpass their personal limitations.

    It's also a sign with a tendency to go overboard. They never do things halfway.

    With an independent nature, this mutable fire sign needs to feel like it can remain free and autonomous no matter what.

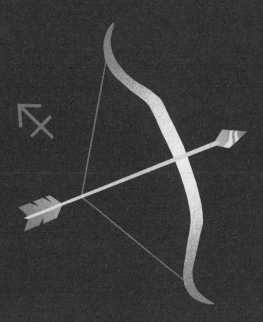

SAGITTARIUS RISING

Life is a big and fabulous adventure to you. You navigate the world while looking for new experiences.

You welcome life with joy and an abundance of energy. As a matter of fact, you are often seen as the life of the party.

With an optimistic nature, you believe your luck will hold no matter what, and you feel protected.

SAGITTARIUS SUN

You are an enthusiastic and optimistic person. You see life on the bright side but be careful: you can sometimes see things through an overly positive lens, which can push you to ignore the problems that may cross your path.

With an attraction for strange and new things, you are here to learn thanks to the many experiences life could bring you.

Your ideal party would take place somewhere on the other side of the world, talking about changing the world with strangers.

SAGITTARIUS MOON

With this placement, you feel a great need for freedom and independence, which is why you hate feeling stuck.

You don't really like having a routine, and much prefer constant renewal.

You also need things to be light and casual, and tend to disconnect away from your upsetting thoughts.

Capricorn

Cardinal earth sign, ruled by Saturn.

As a serious and mature sign, the Capricorn is not here to fool around. They prefer to build solid things.

The Capricorn is a true cardinal earth sign and is thus persevering and determined. But their strategy is very different from the Aries's strategy, always burning with enthusiasm.

The Capricorn is patient and isn't afraid to take things slow, measuring the risks at every step, all the while never giving up.

It's a sign who loves to undertake new things, or at least have things under control.

Overly organized and focused on efficiency and success, the Capricorn can also fall into bad habits and get burned out by work, while getting disconnected from their inner and emotional world.

CAPRICORN RISING

You are pretty reserved, and at first glance you seem very mature and even unapproachable. This placement comes with a "resting bitch face": you don't let anything show through.

You have stable energy levels, and you can have amazing endurance, which explains why you can control your energy, and why you don't easily let your environment affect you. Even when it's stressful or you're under a lot of pressure.

CAPRICORN SUN

You are reliable no matter what, and even when you're hard to reach because of a busy schedule, your loved ones know you can make yourself available when needed.

Your organizational skills and seriousness don't affect your irresistible sense of humor at all. Because even though you try to hide it, you know how to be funny, and can use irony perfectly.

With a Sun in Capricorn, you are also an ambitious person, aspiring to build solid foundations and to climb the social ladder.

CAPRICORN MOON

Even as a child, you were probably very mature, and already showed (as you do today) great seriousness and strictness.

However, this placement can also push you to change and evolve over time, and thus let loose as you grow older.

A Moon in Capricorn doesn't make it easy for you to connect to your emotions. And so, this is a conscious effort you need to start doing to cultivate your emotional intelligence.

Aquarius

Fixed air sign, ruled by the planets Saturn and Uranus.

Aquarius is a paradoxical sign whose energy is both very connected to the invisible and very intellectual: with an Aquarius, you never know what to expect.

Ruled by the Planet Uranus (among other things), Aquarius brings surprise after surprise, and never stops reinventing themselves.

Future-oriented, the Aquarius is the visionary of the zodiac, and they know how to project themselves way beyond what already exists.

The Aquarius is an original sign, who is on this Earth to accept themselves fully, in their uniqueness. They are aware of that, and are even proud of it.

The Aquarius also wants to be greatly invested in causes that are greater than them, and to put their energy in the service of the well-being of their community.

AQUARIUS RISING

You navigate the world in your own personal way, but always with charisma.

You have a unique style, and you hate following trends. You wish to be fully yourself, and to embrace your originality.

Others see you as a friendly, sociable, and sometimes eccentric person, but you tend to keep your distance and avoid getting too invested.

AQUARIUS SUN

You have a great need for freedom and independence.

Learning new things and meeting people are some of what motivates you in life, but you don't let others see through you, and it's hard for other people to really know you. You still often lead your group of friends.

You enjoy shocking others with your eccentricity, of which you are very proud. You love claiming your uniqueness.

You can struggle with authority, and when people tell you what to do, you often feel the need to do the exact opposite.

AQUARIUS MOON

With this placement, you have an extroverted nature, and love social relationships.

You like to dream, and because you're often lost in your own thoughts, you can feel disconnected from your own emotions, which you can sometimes intellectualize.

You think about the future a lot, which can make you anxious at times. If I can give you one piece of advice: ground yourself in the present as much as you can and remind yourself that everything will be okay.

Pisces

Mutable water sign, ruled by the planets Jupiter and Neptune.

We finish this astral journey with Pisces, a soft, romantic, and ethereal sign. Known for being an out-of-step dreamer, Pisces is also the sign of unconditional love.

Pisces want to bring compassion and kindness into the world; it's what motivates them.

They are very connected to spirituality, and can sometimes be in their own thoughts, to the point where they can forget to live in the present.

Pisces are very creative, with an overflowing imagination: they're the artists of the zodiac.

Neptune's energy gives them a pure and radiant aura, which is very attractive to energy vampires of all sorts. Thus, it's important for this sign to learn how to detect toxic people's vibrations, and the people who wish them harm.

PISCES RISING

You are perceived as a soft, deeply nice, and kind person.

Other people can think you are a bit distant and disconnected from this world at times.

Your presence is soothing, even healing, but you are also very sensitive to the energies around you, so remember to protect yourself.

PISCES SUN

Easygoing and easy to live with, you know how to let go and follow the flow of life.

You have a great will to see the good in all things, and you are incredibly nice and kind.

But remember to keep your feet on the ground, and don't believe illusions: you tend to idealize people and situations, to the point where reality can be disappointing. And that's when you may try to run from the real world and hide in your endless daydreaming, sometimes even using substances.

PISCES MOON

You have an oversensitive nature, and you feel everything strongly: emotions easily flow through you, and you are very receptive.

Your creativity is boundless, and you're deeply connected to your artistic side. It's probably the perfect escape for you, the thing that helps you whenever you feel like running away from the real world.

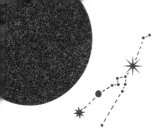

The Houses

ALL RIGHT, now that we have explored the zodiac, we can circle back to the astrological Houses. As I've said earlier, there are twelve Houses, each representing an aspect of life.

To sum up all the things we have covered so far and hopefully make things clearer for you, imagine that the world is the movie set of your life: the rising sign is the role you play, the Sun sign is the actor/actress you are, who is playing this character, and the Houses are the different sets where you are shooting the various movie scenes.

The First House

Linked to the Aries sign and the planet Mars, the first House is the House of your rising sign.

This House is connected to who you are: your identity, your personality, the way you are perceived in this world, but also your physical appearance.

In the first House, we're here to be fully ourselves, and to focus on how to assert our personality.

The Second House

Linked to the Taurus sign and the planet Venus, the second House represents materialistic possessions, everything you obtain, and thus your money.

This House can give you indications on how you can make a living, manage your money as well as your values, but also on your body and your relationship to your body. After all, as soon as we are born, our body is the first thing we truly own.

In the second House, we are here to know what really matters to us, and work on our relationship to all the things we own.

The Third House

Linked to Mercury and the Gemini sign, the third House is the House of sharing information and logic.

It's the House of the intellect, communication, basic learning (knowledge learned in school), but also neighborhood, siblinghood, and short-distance travel.

In the third House, we are here to talk, learn, share, and develop relationships.

The Fourth House

Linked to the Cancer sign and the Moon, the fourth House is the beginning of another important angle in your birth chart: the Bottom of the Sky.

Because of this, the fourth House carries the energy of this angle, and represents the home, the house, the family, and the roots, as well as the ancestral lineage. Because it's associated to the Moon, it can also give information about your subconscious, but also about the way you inhabit your body.

In the fourth House, we feel at home, and we question ourselves about our relationship to family, to our roots, and how we act in private.

The Fifth House

Linked to the Leo sign and the Sun, the fifth House is the House of fun.

It's thus the House of entertaining, children, romance (as we will see later in the book), and creativity.

In the fifth House, we are here to have fun, fall in love, and cultivate our childlike wonder.

The Sixth House

Linked to the Virgo sign and thus to Mercury, the sixth House is the House of health, purity, and our relationship to our body.

With this House, we are back to serious things since it is connected to daily life, routine, work, and organization.

In the sixth House, we live our daily life, we work, and we are responsible.

The Seventh House

Always the opposite of the first House, the seventh House is the descendant House. Thus, it represents the opposite of the first House (which is focused on you) and focuses on others.

Linked to the Libra and Venus, it's the House of contracts, associations, and partnerships (including love partnerships).

Yes, the seventh House is the House of relationships in general, but the heart of this House is still love, since this is traditionally the House of marriage.

In the seventh House, we connect to others, and we learn to know more about ourselves thanks to others.

The Eighth House

As the opposite of the second House, the eighth House represents our relationship to the immaterial, the intangible.

Linked to the Scorpio sign and the planets Mars and Pluto, this House represents intimacy, sexuality, the occult, and everything that is hidden and taboo, which includes our secrets.

The eighth House is also the House of other people's money, meaning inheritance, investments, and banks.

In the eighth House, we dive deep, we reclaim our darkest sides, and we connect intimately.

The Ninth House

As the opposite of the third House (basic learning and logic), the ninth House is the House of academic studies, university, philosophy, religion, and spirituality.

Linked to the Sagittarius sign and the planet Jupiter, the ninth House is also the House of travels, adventure, and exploration. Thus, it also symbolizes all that is foreign and distant.

In the ninth House, we go on a faraway journey, we show spontaneity, and we change the world with people we had never even met the day before.

The Tenth House

If its opposite, the fourth House, tells you where you're from, the tenth House represents where you are going and who you will become.

Linked to the Capricorn and Saturn, the tenth House is another essential angle in your birth chart: the Midheaven.

Unlike the sixth House that represents everyday work, the tenth House is the House of your career throughout your life, but also of your reputation and your social status.

In the tenth House, we accomplish ourselves socially, we build, and we are careful about our reputation.

The Eleventh House

Linked to the Aquarius, Saturn, and Uranus, the eleventh House is the House of connections, whether it is connections to others, or to technological things.

It's the House of friendship and community, but also the House of technologies, social media, and the Internet.

This House is also the House of astrology; it represents being avant-garde and having a visionary mind.

In the eleventh House, we commit to a cause and to the collective, and we look further away, even if it means already stepping a foot into the future.

The Twelfth House

Finally, the twelfth House. This House is probably the most complicated to understand since it groups together all the energies of the other Houses.

Linked to the Pisces sign and the planets Jupiter and Neptune, this House is a place of spiritual connection.

It's the House of the invisible, the intangible, and the irrational, but it's also connected to enclosed places where one can feel lonely, like hospitals (psychiatric or not) and prisons. It's also linked to the challenges of life, and the end of a cycle.

In the twelfth House, we face ourselves, we contemplate, and we connect ourselves to something greater.

I think you now have all the basics to understand the energy of your birth chart. If you haven't discovered it as you read, I invite you to do so. Then, I suggest you take a little break, so you can focus on how you feel now that you have learned all these things about yourself. If you want, you can take your Astro notebook, so you can write down how you feel.

This first part comes to an end. We will meet again later in the third part, in which I will address more precisely the astrological analysis of each placement, and their connection to love and sexuality. I will focus on the energies of Venus, Mars, and the fifth, seventh, and eighth Houses to explain more precisely what they represent and what they tell you about love and sexuality.

If you wish to know more about your birth chart in general, I recommend you follow me on Instagram and listen to the podcast I created, which will give you a lot of fascinating information. But for now: *let's talk about sex, baby!*

2

sex & love

How I See
Sex Coaching

PSYCHOLOGISTS AND COACHES are two drastically different professions. Psychologists have a degree in psychology, which allows them to study human behavior to help their patients solve their psychological struggles in the long term. Coaches, on the other hand, can have various trainings and specialties, and will offer you varied tools to work on your present and/or your future in a tangible and immediate way.

As a coach myself, I use a lot of self-development tools to help the amazing people I help, according to a method called "holistic." I believe in the little things in life, the enlightenment that very different subjects can bring us (even quantum physics at times!) to guide us, without us even realizing it.

I was always interested in astrology, and I deeply believe in it. That is why I love using it during my sessions. It's also why I was impatient to work with Amina to write this book: she allows me to connect to this field even more.

On top of guiding people in their spirituality, I also help them build healthy romantic relationships, and I guide them toward a fulfilling sex life. Being a sex coach means helping people (re)build their sexuality, whether by teaching them basic knowledge about sexual intercourse, or by guiding them toward deconstructing their limiting beliefs so they can live a kind and cohesive sex life. For example, I host fellatio and cunnilingus online trainings to teach my community how to ground themselves in these practices.

I am also currently studying clinical sexology. Thanks to this training, I am learning more about health, since we are taught certain illnesses linked to sexuality.

I honestly believe that my job is a blessing to me: I'm so happy to see people smiling at the end of a coaching session. It's amazing! So, if you need to hear this today: yes, you can turn your passion into a job, and make a living from it. And remember, your birth chart can give you clues to help you in that endeavor.

As you probably understand by now, I am passionate about my job, and thanks to astrology, I always know I'm right where I should be, even when I'm faced with challenges. I am a Virgo Sun, and I have placements that match my job. To me, it's as if it was written. As if, since the first time I drew breath, my life path was already written in me.

And now, let me take you on a journey to explore the vast world of love and sexuality.

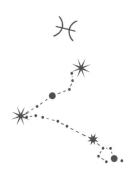

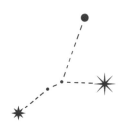

Romantic Relationships

THE MAIN TOPIC of this book is the strong connection between sexuality and astrology. But I find it important to also talk about love, to talk about healthy relationships and compatibility, among other things.

Leaving Toxicity Behind

Before we can go any further, it seems essential to me to define the concepts of toxic relationships and healthy relationships. A healthy relationship is based on many elements which, once assembled, make us feel good with someone else.

But before I can speak more in depth about this, I must admit something. I am a coach, and yet, I used to be toxic. It's important to me that you know that, for the sake of honesty. Actually, everyone has some toxic behaviors. These behaviors take different shapes: an overly strong jealousy, a constant need to test other people's love, the desire to control others . . . The only thing that matters is trying to work on these things throughout our life.

We are constantly evolving, and every day is a new step. So, if you have already behaved in a toxic way in a past relationship, I would like you to take the time to forgive yourself. Because for you to change your behavior, you first need to acknowledge it, and to be able to be kind about these behaviors you had at some point in your life. It all starts there.

Furthermore, if you think you're behaving in a toxic way right now, I can only advise you to start therapy with a psychologist. It really helped me question myself, analyze the patterns I had fallen victim to, and to understand why I protected myself like that, by being toxic in return. It seems to me that it's the only way to move on to healthy relationships.

Take the time you need and be patient: it can be a long journey. As for me, it took me a while to forgive myself. I hated myself, and was sure everyone hated me too, that everyone was ganging up on me. I had to fight to find myself.

I am a North African woman, and today, even though I was toxic, I am on my own path, at the conquest of love and sexuality. I am proud of it. I wish you to also feel proud of who you are, but this requires you to work on yourself. Admitting we have toxic behaviors and seeing a therapist are the first steps. You can also keep a journal to follow your evolution.

I also want you to understand something important. If you realize you're behaving in a toxic way, or are being treated in a toxic way, it's probably time for you to step away and cut ties with the relevant person(s).

In the first case, you have certainly hurt the people to whom you were toxic, and you can't be reborn next to them. A separation is unavoidable so you can change and grow with guidance, without ever giving up. If you don't do it, you might ruin all your friendships and romantic relationships.

If you are a victim of toxic behavior, it's essential that you protect yourself. You deserve a healthy relationship based on attentiveness, sharing, and kindness.

The Pillars of a
Healthy Relationship

Here are the essential pillars to build a healthy relationship:
- The possibility to truly be yourself
- Implementing non-negotiable things, aka boundaries
- A clear and kind communication
- Being free to express your emotions
- No emotional abuse (which should happen naturally if the following pillars are strong)

I am going to make you discover these pillars by explaining to you how to achieve them, and I'll give you tips as well as little writing exercises.

☾ Knowing How to Be Genuine

Be yourself.

Our society forces us to wear different masks according to the context, to be validated by others or to desperately fit into the mold. And yet it is essential for you to truly be yourself. Thus, you need to be in a relationship that allows you to express your personality, your humor, and your passions, without any judgment.

When you like someone, don't try to change to be accepted by them. The need for validation is something we all feel to some extent. Who has never wanted to be liked by others, thinking it will help them feel better in their own skin?

But you need to accept yourself as you are. Because the people who love you genuinely love you for who you are, not who you are pretending to be.

Moreover, if you're building a relationship while playing a part, it will at most last a few months before your mask starts cracking and your true personality seeps through. It's indeed impossible to suffocate who we are for too long. Even in little things, your deep nature will manifest to free itself from the part you forced on it. Worse, if you persist you might lose parts of yourself just to please every new crush.

You're not to blame, though. It's only natural to want to seduce someone we like. And it's even truer in our society, where validation fuels us. However, if you want to be honest with yourself, you will need to escape from the patterns that society forces on us to build a healthy relationship.

For example, if you are a woman or present as a woman, you don't have to act like a soft and loving woman to appeal to others. And if you are a man or identify as a man, you don't need to be manly and hide your emotions to seduce someone.

As a coach, I often see relationships being destroyed by "toxic masculinity." Toxic masculinity is defined by the "manly" behavior stereotypes, aka the endless motto "men are strong, harsh, manly." It completely blocks their emotional center. If you are dating a man, don't hesitate to show him that he can steer clear of these norms to show himself as he is. The patriarchy oppresses women, but it also impacts men.

Everyone is different, and we find our inner magic in our uniqueness. Try journaling, for example. Each night, in a notebook or on your computer, write what you're going through and how you feel, to slowly connect to who you really are.

Because the real secret to seducing someone is to truly be yourself. This is how you will attract relationships that align with yourself, because it is the true you that will have seduced the other person.

☾ Communicating with Kindness

Once you have acknowledged your inner beauty, you will be able to strive toward kind, sincere, and genuine communication. In a healthy relationship, communication is key. I myself took a course on nonviolent communication, and I use it daily.

It's an extraordinary tool. It allows you to learn how to say "thank you" more often, how to be grateful and careful, how not to give unasked advice, to actively listen to others and pay attention to details, to have a healthy and genuine relationship.

Communication—whether it is verbal or nonverbal—is a driving force for all human beings. We constantly use it, and it's the tool that allows us to create deeper bonds. But because of the way love is perceived in our society, we often feel like we must filter what we want to share with someone else. I call this "society's love education."

Society has taught us codes on love that we have internalized and now apply without thinking. It has a great impact on romantic behaviors and our sexuality. For example, many women in heterosexual relationships believe they can't have sex on the first night, for fear of being branded an "easy lay." It is as problematic as it is unfair, and it is a prejudice created by society.

These codes have taught us how to communicate a certain way; they have led us to believe that screaming and fighting is normal; and that we should always sort out what we want to share or not, for fear of hurting our partner.

But there is an essential element to take into consideration to communicate effectively: knowing how to listen is the basis of any exchange. When someone is telling you something, sharing something with you, try to really receive the message without any judgment. Just welcome it and wait for the right time to answer. It's important to reply kindly, without guilting the other person or making them regret sharing.

If someone wants to tell you something and you're not available, it's better to tell them upfront than to pretend to listen. For example, I can sometimes say, "I'm sorry, but I'm really busy right now. Do you mind if we talk about this later? I would rather listen to you 100 percent." This simple sentence will avoid a lot of misunderstanding, because in general, if you're not really listening to someone, they will notice, and things might explode between you. So, stating your boundaries in your exchanges and your relationships is very important.

Communicating can also mean rephrasing what someone has just told you. If you're not sure you understand what the other person is trying to express, don't hesitate to rephrase their words to make sure you've got it right. And if you want to keep talking to someone, remember to ask open questions to know more about them and their life. This will nourish the conversation!

amal's communication advice
1. Be available and listen.
2. State your boundaries if you aren't available.
3. Be genuine and share your true feelings.
4. Rephrase if you're not sure you understand.
5. Ask open questions.

Remember that communication will help you build a strong relationship. You need to learn from the start how to ask questions like "What's wrong? Do you want to talk about it?" It's one of the pillars on which you will build a healthy relationship.

☾ Knowing How to Recognize Your Green Flags and Red Flags

We all have green flags and red flags that we need to keep in mind whenever we pick our dates, to know where we're going when we meet someone. Of course, they can vary according to people, and you need to know yours.

Our green flags are the things that make us feel safe, the reassuring things that validate our emotional needs. Red flags are all those things that stop you from liking the person in front of you.

Here are some examples of green flags and red flags:

GREEN FLAGS	RED FLAGS
Active listening	Negating your emotions
Protected life space	Omnipresence
Genuine desire to know how you live, your loved ones	Judging you and your loved ones
Respecting your boundaries	Guilt-tripping
Valorization, congratulations, and encouragement	Depreciation

Your turn! I suggest you take your Astro notebook to make the list of your own green flags and red flags. You can draw inspiration from the table above.

☾ Recognizing and Expressing Your Emotions

The last point I would like to address about romantic relationships is about expressing emotions.

In our society, there is a reserve toward showcasing emotions. Do you see what I mean? Showing our emotions, especially so-called "negative" emotions such as sadness, means being vulnerable. And there is this deeply rooted belief that vulnerability is a weakness. It's the reason why, when you see someone crying, you're uncomfortable and will often undermine their pain and try to comfort them so they stop. Even if you mean well, it might not be the best thing to do.

As a matter of fact, we have a rather conflictual relationship with "negative" emotions in the West. Many don't allow them to flow, and we often refuse to live them fully. And yet, it is essential to try not to suppress and interiorize them. These reactions might prevent you from dealing with the emotions, and they might stay stuck inside you, only to explode later.

When you feel a so-called "positive" emotion like joy, you will usually savor it and allow it to spread inside you. It eventually leaves to return later. You do it spontaneously and naturally because society accepts "positive" emotions.

However, "negative" emotions are not accepted. Yet, they need to travel through us before they can leave, just like "positive" emotions. When I say "travel," I mean that you need to live them in full conscience. To use the example of joy again: whenever you feel joy, you allow yourself to laugh and even weep with joy. Thus, you express joy without a second thought. Well, whenever you are feeling an uncomfortable emotion, the goal is to be able to do the same thing, which means letting it travel through you and manifest itself.

When starting a relationship, it's important to be honest with yourself (and your partner) and to express your emotions genuinely. I can only advise you to allow yourself to be vulnerable in front of this person: dare to cry, show your fear, your sadness, or even your anger. All these emotions are important. They exist within you, and thus are legitimate and you are allowed to share them.

If you are seeing someone who always minimizes, denies, or ridicules your emotions, I suggest you reconsider your relationship. In the long term, it could push you to totally repress your emotions.

Finally, I believe that there are not "negative" or "positive" emotions. There are only emotions with which you are either comfortable or not. Emotions are subjective. According to your education and your experiences, you will experience them differently. What matters is to accept them. If an emotion is making you uncomfortable, try not to block it. Instead, try to set it free by setting up a ritual, for example, to live it and allow it to travel through you. Little by little, you will learn to manage this emotion.

At this stage of the book, I invite you to use your Astro notebook to think about emotions and your relationship to them. You can do it as a table, divided in two columns: one with the emotions you feel comfortable with, and the other with emotions that make you uncomfortable. Main emotions are joy, anger, fear, sadness, disgust, and surprise. But you can do this exercise using the various sentiments derived from them: love, compassion, melancholy, disdain, nostalgia . . .

I hope this exercise allows you to learn more about yourself. I believe that in the end, whether we are talking about astrology, love, or sexuality, the goal in life is to meet ourselves, to ground within ourselves, aligning and adjusting when needed.

I am, by the way, sure that this is exactly what bonds us with Amina: guiding others toward self-fulfillment. Because whether we are talking about love, sexuality, or our birth chart, we are talking about the essence of human beings. We are talking about you, your soul, and your energetic body. This is what interests us.

I have given you the pillars that help build healthy relationships. You can obviously find others because interpersonal relationships are complicated and multidimensional. But now that you have all these bases in mind, it is time to explore your sexuality.

Leaving Mainstream Sexuality

a little warning Be careful, talking about sexuality may reveal some mental blocks, and can even make trauma resurface, whether it is conscious or unconscious trauma. If you have trauma, I encourage you to turn to a mental health professional. It is essential to work on your trauma, and this is beyond coaching. Mental health professionals (psychologists, psychiatrists, or therapists) are the only people who can help and guide you down this path.

IN THE NEXT PART, we will talk about your hot, sensual, or sexual placements. But before that, I would like to talk more generally about your sexuality to help you go all the way, always further. Just like you dug deep in the previous section, with everything about astrology that Amina explained to you even if it wasn't directly connected to sexuality, I now would like to help you discover aspects of sexuality that have nothing to do with astrology. It's important for me to know that you will close this book feeling more connected to your sexuality.

Sexuality is a delicate thing to talk about. It's a form of communication, just like verbal and nonverbal language. And in our everyday life, actions, people, and words influence our sexual language, which I will decipher to allow you to go beyond patterns that can be toxic.

Sexuality and Mainstream Pornography

Mainstream and "penetrocentric" pornography undeniably impact us. From a very young age, we base our sexual education on an unrealistic, misogynistic, racist, and heteronormative sexuality, which disrespects sex workers and teaches us that there is only one way to have sexual intercourse. Sex without penetration is nonexistent, feminine pleasure is totally erased, and consent is ridiculed.

> **penetrocentric: what does it mean?** The word *penetrocentric* means "focused on penetration." A penetrocentric sexuality or society sees penetration as the ultimate goal of sexual intercourse. And so, in mainstream porn, for example, penetration is the focus of the sexual act, and everything revolves around it (script and cameras alike).

In mainstream porn movies and websites, the showcasing of only one way to live one's sexuality, without having really any other choice, is terribly reductive. It's probably why you may feel limited, or maybe even oppressed and suffocated in your sexuality: you've always only been offered one way.

If people keep trying to educate themselves through this unethical media, it's mostly because parents and children don't talk about sexuality, and the notion of pleasure, sexual orientation, and gender are never discussed in school. Even if parents aren't the only ones responsible for a child's education—since society, school, teachers, and classmates largely contribute to it too—they are essential to the sexual construction of children, and the anatomical knowledge they can develop.

Even today, sexuality is a very powerful taboo, a subject people don't talk about, instead just hiding it under the rug because it is, among other things, seen as dirty and impure. But sexuality is part of human relationships, and there is not only one way to express ourselves sexually through our body and our partner's body.

Sexuality and Activism

These mainstream porn platforms' success is the direct result of the taboo we have about sexuality in our society. Sex workers are professional, working an actual job, and they deserve to work safely. Unfortunately, these mainstream websites prevent them from having a safe workspace environment that would allow them to work in decent and humane conditions.

As you may have noticed, my feminist beliefs and my activism are deeply connected to the way I see sexuality. It is impossible for me to talk about sex without talking about these essential subjects, because to me there is no way around them if you want to blossom and grow in your sexuality, and so you can also have a good sexual health.

It so happens that the sexuality of women and minorities—meaning people who don't belong to the dominating group, whether we are talking about origins, religion, gender, or sexual orientation—has been largely oppressed by patriarchy, racism, or the demonization of sex education. Instead of allowing women to live their sexuality freely, and blossom through it, Western society has constantly and violently forbidden them pleasure, and has prevented them from feeling comfortable in this aspect of their lives by encouraging feelings of guilt and worry. This is also the case for other minorities, with the fetishization of racialized bodies, the sexualization of lesbian sex through the male gaze, or other forms of systemic sexual oppression linked to gender or sexual orientation.

So, on top of sexual taboo—which, as we've seen earlier, creates a lot of gaps in our sexual education—there is this social phenomenon that unscrupulously oppresses women and minorities' sexuality.

And yet, sexuality is a natural thing. It is truly part of human nature. If you want to learn more about this, I invite you to follow my Instagram account, and to read my first book (*Bien Dans Ma Tête, Bien Dans Ma Culotte!* Kiwi 2020, available only in French). There are also plenty of other Instagram accounts and books that answer the questions you may ask yourself about all this. Because even if our relationship to sexuality is still not perfect, things are changing: information is circulating and getting richer, and words are breaking the taboo. By the way, we suggest many books and Instagram accounts at the end of this book!

Even though this book's purpose is not sexual education per se, its goal is nonetheless to guide you toward your right to pleasure. Learning to know yourself sexually thanks to the stars can allow you to connect more deeply to your inner Self and your sexuality, and find fulfillment in pleasure.

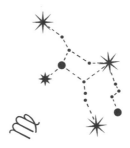

Positive Sexuality

Learning to Know Yourself Through Sexuality

As you will quickly notice, I see sexuality as something at the crossroads between clinical sexuality and spiritual sexuality, both grounded and conscious. It is thus multidimensional.

What is amazing is that there are as many sexualities as there are people. The way we see sexuality is influenced by our culture, our education, our beliefs, our fears, our trauma . . . For example, the concept of a "first time" is different for everyone. Some people find it very important, others don't. Some people see their first time as the first time they had a sexual experience (with penetration or not), and for others, it's vaginal or anal penetration that determines a first time.

It seems to me that one of the fundamental pillars of a fulfilling sexuality is the practice of something called "positive sexuality." Positive sexuality is a way to envision sexuality that puts pleasure and consent at the center of one's sexual relationships, and that develops one's five senses to live a peaceful, limitless, fearless, open, and fulfilling sexuality.

What I like about positive sexuality is that, just like astrology, it regroups the four elements: fire with sexual passion; water with cleansing sexual energy; air, which allows us to feel "high" during sex (meaning the feeling of freedom enhanced by endorphins); and the grounding earth. But on top of the four elements, this vision also sees sexuality as warm and cold, winter and summer, black and white, "feminine" and "masculine" energy.

Furthermore, if there is one thing I have learned as a neuroscience coach specializing in positive sexuality, it's that our sexuality is not a straight line, nor is it something limited and simple. It's a learning curve, a path that we explore, where we can stumble, find ourselves, and evolve.

In my opinion, it's just like libido: you don't have just one way to live your libido, but multiple ways. And you might not always have the same libido level, and it's unnecessary to try to put yourself in a box, because you can totally live with the flow of your body. And yet there are so many stereotypes about libido: men's libido is presumably higher, which is why men who sleep with many women are praised (while we all know how women who sleep with many men are treated); some women are thought to be frigid; and some might think pregnant women lose their libido.

This is obviously all false. There is no correlation between libido and biological sex. However, there is clearly a correlation between libido and society. Men don't actually have *more* libido, they are just more allowed to express it, since a man having frequent sexual intercourse is validated by society. Society coins him as a Casanova, a successful man. It's much more complicated for women because the codes are not the same.

But to live your sexuality fully, you need to set yourself free from the injunctions and the stereotypes. And so, I will guide you so you can align to the positive sexuality frequency, which corresponds to what I believe to be the true and deep sexuality, the sexuality that is a bit holy, away from the mainstream and penetrocentric porn that warp, sometimes even destroy, our bodily and sexual patterns.

You now understand that sexuality is an aspect of life that can tell a lot about you, and that can allow you to learn more about your fears, your mental blocks, and your needs. Even today, people see sexuality as "just sex" when it can be a whole world to discover; this personal path can allow you to find yourself, to open up and walk toward fulfillment.

When you begin to understand your own sexuality, when you see sexuality as something sacred and you manage to meet your energy and your sexual power, you automatically become a more grounded person. You are here. You are present. Because, again, positive sexuality is sacred and is both a quest for pleasure and self-development.

It's also important to remember that sexuality is a moment to share bodies, memories, and pleasure. If you are in the middle of sexual intercourse and aren't feeling any pleasure, the best thing is to tell your partner. So gather your courage and express how you feel, because you aren't obligated to feel pleasure. Sometimes you think you're in the mood, and then you realize you aren't. Sometimes you're too worried about other things and you can't enjoy the sexual act. And sometimes, your partner isn't doing things the way you like them, and it's then essential to say it so the relationship can evolve.

Your sexuality evolves at the same time as your soul.

Just like astrology is a tool for self-development, I see sexuality as an inner journey, a way to meditate about yourself, about the feelings circulating within you.

If you're asking yourself what counts as being something sexual in this book, know that it includes all sensual things: kisses, looks, hugs, skin to skin contact, but also of course cunnilingus, fellatio,

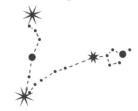

vaginal or anal penetration . . . all these things are a part of sexuality. Not just penetration.

We are not talking here about a penetrocentric or a heteronormative sexuality, and that's for two main reasons. Firstly, as we've said, penetration is not an end in itself. It is only one sexual act among many other possibilities to experiment with your sexuality. Secondly, sexual intercourse isn't just something done by people respectively having a penis and a vagina. Moreover, all sexual orientations exist and are welcome here.

Now I invite you to take your Astro notebook and answer the following question: How do you live your sexuality outside penetration? This exercise will allow you to realize your relationship to sexuality once penetration is taken out of the equation. Writing down how you feel about a sexual act without penetration will allow you to understand what place penetration has in your sex life, if and how you like it, why it's important or not for you, why you need it, and how you would live your sexuality if penetration wasn't a part of it. It could allow you to imagine a different sexuality from the one you usually know.

Consent

No matter how you practice sexuality (how, where, with whom, when, etc.), it is essential for consent to be the priority. It is the starting point of any intense, real, and healthy sexual intercourse. Without consent, this isn't safe sex at all since it becomes sexual assault. Consent was denied and disrespected for a long time; it was silenced by everyday violence, but it is ESSENTIAL.

To be clear, there are no sexualities "with consent" or "without consent." There is only sexual intercourse or sexual assault. Before starting any sexual act, it is essential to ask if the person consents, and to share your own consent with them.

No, it won't ruin the moment. On the contrary, the safety of the act can only exist after both people say yes. So, it's even better. I believe that it's even the only way to have sex and try new things. And even if someone says yes for one thing, and you want to try something else, it's always best to ask for their consent. You don't know someone else's story, and you can't know what they want to do or not until you've asked them.

There are different ways to ask if someone consents or not:
- "Can I . . . ?"
- "Do you want to do it?"
- "Are you fine with this? I am, but your consent is important."

Once the other person's consent is guaranteed, you can check they still consent at any time you want during the sexual act:
- "Is everything okay?"
- "Are you feeling well?"
- "Are you still fine? Don't hesitate to tell me if you want to stop. You're free to tell me, it's your body."

Most importantly, if the person says no, you should never insist with words or action, or by guilt-tripping them. It is extremely violent for your partner. Guilt-tripping someone during sex is overstepping the boundaries of safe sex and can be very traumatizing for the person exposed to it.

Never negotiate a no: no means no.

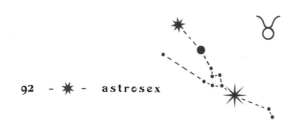

Sexuality Is a Journey

THIS IS AN ESSENTIAL THING to accept: your sexuality will evolve throughout your life. Just like your birth chart's interpretation will be affected by what you're living at any given point, you will experience your sexuality differently according to your path and evolution.

Amina talked about this in the previous part: every astrologer will read different things in you with the same birth chart. Well, it's kind of the same thing here: every partner, every sexual act will bring you specific feelings that will give you many ways to understand yourself. This stems from the fact that no sexual act is identical, and you'll never feel the same thing: ambience can change, just like acts and sexual positions, and you will progressively discover new things. You will slowly learn to know yourself better, to know what your likes and dislikes are. But even this will constantly change throughout your life.

For example, when we start becoming more confident, we live our sexuality very differently. When we are self-conscious, we obviously struggle to fully immerse in the sexual act. We can often believe our partner is a gift from life, and that we don't deserve them in a way. Moreover, when we aren't very self-confident in general, we don't like our bodies and thus we struggle to let go during the sexual act.

But don't worry, you can work on this: sexual confidence doesn't appear out of nowhere, especially in our society, which doesn't guide us toward acceptance and self-love. Because, yes, our body is one of the centers of sexuality (the other being the brain, the emotional center), and for it to be aware during sexual acts, we need to love it. It can take time; this is also a journey.

And all these things are the reasons that make me believe that there is not such a thing as a "good" or "bad" lay. How we brand and hierarchize people is yet another way to pressure ourselves and others, in a society that already pushes us to put ourselves in boxes and label ourselves.

In reality, there are sexual connections that happen more easily than others: it might be easier for you to let go with one person but not with another. There's no explanation really. It either works or it doesn't. For some people connection is important, and they really need to learn to know one another, to masturbate next to each other to observe, and it's perfectly normal.

You are constantly evolving, just like everyone else. You work on your mental blocks, your fears, your self-confidence. Sexuality is also a way for you to grow, to be fulfilled within your Self and your being. This is the right moment to ask yourself if you crave other people's validation, and if yes, why or how. You can also ask yourself how your masturbation practices are connected to your self-confidence and self-esteem. As for your relationship to others, it is also unveiled through sexuality. That is why I invite you to think of sexuality as something fun and hot, but also transformative and powerful.

Sexuality Without Penetration

SEXUALITY WITHOUT PENETRATION allows your body to step away from our society's norms, but also to ground yourself in a new way to experience sexuality. It will also stimulate your creativity when it comes to sexuality, because you will look for other ways to feel or give pleasure, which will help you step out of your comfort zone.

You can let yourself be engrossed by glances, the eye contacts that connect. Eyes are the windows to the soul, and creating this visual connection in your sexuality will allow you to fully live your sexual acts.

Another way is the exploration of manual sex, thanks to different caresses that you can deploy on all parts of the body. Look for a quiver, this feeling that is born in your abdomen and spreads to your lips, because looking for the physical feelings that society denied us is also what it means to make love.

Using your mouth is another way to feel and give sexual pleasure. You can give your partner pleasure by kissing their body, and oral sex is a sexual practice in its own right, which you can absolutely decide to explore more. It is, however, important for you to understand that its purpose isn't to "arouse" your partner. The point is to make love to them, to take the time to use your lips, tongue, and mouth to offer them new sensations.

In the end, every part of your body can be sexual if you decide so. I insist: if and when you decide so, because I believe that you decide whether your body—or a part of it—is sexual. You also decide when you want to be sexualized. Nobody else—especially not men in the street, for example—can decide for you.

In any case, you don't need to penetrate or be penetrated to say you're having sexual intercourse. You define what you see as sexual intercourse, and it's when you want, however you want it.

What really matters is that you learn to know yourself, to know what you like, what excites you and what doesn't. I call that "determining your sexual profile." It's not fixed since it will transform with your experiences and throughout your life. And it might even change with this book, since Amina and I will use the stars to guide you toward your sexuality, so you may discover more about yourself and learn to awaken your sexual energy.

What is your sexual profile? A sexual profile is like an evolutive ID, allowing you to determine what you like or dislike, to figure out how you want to live your sexuality. This profile can help you introduce yourself to others, because communication is the best lubricant there is. I'm inviting you to establish your profile on your Astro notebook. For example: you can use it to write down how your romantic dates went, to analyze your behavior and your relationship to love, and to write about your sexual experiences. Once you do that, don't hesitate to get back to it occasionally to add details and allow it to evolve, but also to look at it with a fresh set of eyes and analyze yourself. And I can only encourage you to share your sexual desires with your partners, and to share your reluctances, too. Talking about these things will allow you to truly live your sexuality in a healthy and serene way.

Orgasm Is Not an End in Itself

IF THERE IS ONE PRINCIPLE I care about deeply in positive sexuality, it's the idea that orgasm is not the ultimate goal of the sexual act.

And by the way, I would like to specify a vocabulary issue: no one ever passively waits to "get" an orgasm, and no one "gives" you an orgasm. You take an orgasm if you want to. It's a pleasure you obtain by guiding the other so they can lead you toward your orgasm, and everyone has a different way to reach it.

Unfortunately, orgasm is often described as a major part of sex in our society's sex education. For a lot of people, it's what determines the quality of a sexual act. Even worse, in heterosexual relationships, a woman reaching orgasm is expected to show gratitude toward her partner: aka, if she had an orgasm, it means her partner is a "good lay" and she should be grateful. This all needs to be deconstructed in my opinion.

The way I see it, if the orgasm is the culmination of physical pleasure, it doesn't mean sexuality is limited to the experience of the physical body. It's just as intense lived intellectually, spiritually, or through the energetic body. Physical orgasm is not the only thing to take into consideration to enjoy the quality of a sexual act.

It's also important to understand there are many reasons someone can't orgasm: stress, a bad day, intrusive thoughts, menstruation, and even more.

You should also know that when you're having sex with your partner, focusing only on the physical orgasm as something that should absolutely be reached won't allow your brain to enjoy the sensuality of the act and the pleasure. If you only focus on the orgasm, without allowing your brain and your cells to feel every ounce of pleasure, it will be actually harder to reach orgasm.

you want to orgasm? here are a few words of advice:
- Let the intense sensations overwhelm you.
- Slow the motions to feel things better (see Slow Sex, page 100).
- If you can't let go, you can ask the person to hug you and enjoy the feeling, without going any further.
- Write a letter to your orgasm to learn more about your mental blocks and your fears.
- Write your fantasies.
- Take the time for solitary pleasures.
- Watch ethical pornography.

The Pleasure of Sex Toys

I'M TAKING ADVANTAGE of the orgasm subject to talk to you about sex toys. In the last part of the book, Amina and I had a great time pairing a sex toy with each zodiac sign, according to their characteristics. It was a lot of fun, but before that I would like to linger over the sex toys phenomenon.

In the last decade, the use of sex toys became popularized. I must admit that I love this generalization, and I find it incredible that these toys are so easily accessible.

However, I remain wary, and I wouldn't advise you to use sex toys too often. In the end, these toys were created to help us reach orgasm quickly. To give you an example, people use sex toys like that: they buy a clitoridean sex toy to climax fast. And using them this way can make us overlook the gradual increase of all the sensations we feel in our body and mind when masturbating or having sex.

I believe it would be more relevant to use these toys as accessories that allow us to awaken the senses, as something to play with during sex, but without giving them too much importance. Because they can also create a habituation to the intense sensations they can give: people get used to it and then they can struggle to climax without it. Orgasm then becomes mechanical and is simply the body's response to a very powerful stimulation no one can imitate.

Slow Sex

SLOW SEX IS A WAY to live your sexuality that was developed in the United States. This movement slowly reached French-speaking countries, and now most professionals such as doctors, sexologists, psychologists, and sex coaches know about slow sex.

If there was a slogan for slow sex, it would go a little bit like this: "Slowing down to better feel." In practice, slow sex is done through soft and slow motions that can be applied on the clitoris, the penis, the anus, or the labia. In reality, slow sex can be done on all parts of the body, without any limits, and more so on the body parts we aren't used to exploring—like the arms, where one can, for example, softly brush their lips.

Slow sex allows you to reach a conscious sexuality. The conscious and subconscious are psychological and psychoanalytical concepts that are used to describe the human life experiences. If the conscious is connected to our ability to take into consideration what we live and feel, the subconscious is used to describe what evades the conscious.

Everyone has a consciousness and, buried in the depth of the mind, a subconscious. Many coping mechanisms come from our

subconscious, as well as reflexes tied to what we have assimilated throughout our life. These things evade our conscious willpower, they're spontaneously set in motion, and sometimes when having sex, we can do things automatically and not take the other person into consideration. Motions can then become too fast—like men stimulating the clitoris too quickly—and sensations dissipate, which will lead to a considerable loss of energy, preventing people from living their sexual life in full consciousness.

And yet, slowing down allows us to feel each breath, each motion, each finger. We feel everything more consciously and thus more intensely. Nothing is ignored and nothing is done subconsciously.

It's exactly like eating a meal. Specialists all say that eating too fast, without chewing, will prevent you from feeling full. This also stems from eating unconsciously (that is also why specialists don't recommend eating in front of the TV or a phone). Well, it's the same thing with sexuality!

> **a little exercise to try slow sex** With the tip of your fingers, a feather, or another soft object, slowly and gently caress your body or your partner's body. Observe their reactions or yours, and let the shivers engulf you. And if after that you want to move to a penetrative act, do it slowly, enjoying every softness.

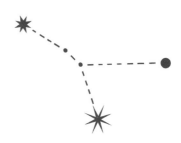

Sexual Energy

ACCORDING TO CERTAIN BELIEFS, sexual energy is like a ball of energy located in the private parts of the body. This energy is always boiling and can spread to the stomach, but it should be differentiated from excitement or sexual desire. It's called "sexual energy," but it can be used for whatever you want, like accomplishing a project or making money.

It's advantageous to learn about this energy, so you can cultivate and ground it. To this end, you need to unite consciousness, slowness, tantric massage, and fusion with your partner. And if you want to use sex toys, pick glass toys over vibrating ones. Cultivating this sexual energy will enhance creativity, spontaneity, and excitement over the little things in life.

> **climaxing in full consciousness** When you feel the orgasm growing, don't restrict it to one place (aka your private parts), instead allowing it to navigate and to climb the seven energetic planes of your beings. The seven energetic planes are the seven chakras: root, sacral, solar plexus, heart, throat, third eye, and crown. Imagine this energy ball climbing stair after stair through the seven planes of your body.

After this (re)discovery of your sexuality, Amina and I will unveil what astrology can bring to your romantic and sexual journey. Like we said before, astrology, love, and sexuality all perfectly and softly mix together and can help you align yourself and find the answers you are looking for.

The next part of this book will give you, among other things, more information about your Venus and Mars placement to reveal what the stars say about you when it comes to love and sexuality. Ready to learn more about you (or about your crush)?

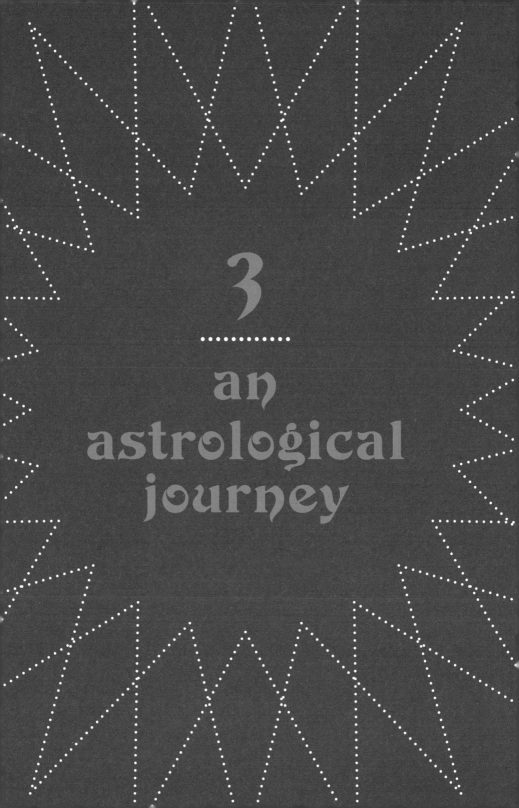

3

an
astrological
journey

Beyond Your Solar Sign

VENUS'S SYMBOL: ♀   MARS'S SYMBOL: ♂

We will now explore together the softness of Venus and the intensity of Mars to learn more about love and sexuality. As you know, a part of my work happens on social media, and I get countless DMs from people sending me their solar sign and the solar sign of their partners, to know if they are compatible.

I'm pretty sure that if you like astrology, you've already wondered whether you and your crush have compatible signs. And I imagine that when you see posts about astrology on your Instagram feed, you have both your solar signs in mind to check what the stars are saying. Who hasn't?

If you've ever asked yourself this question, or if you're currently wondering, know that you can't calculate an astrological love compatibility with the Sun sign only. It's too reductive. To seriously analyze and understand astrological love compatibility, we need to do something called "synastry."

Synastry simply consists of the superposition of two birth charts, to study them in relation to each other. Well, I say "simply," but it's actually very complex. I can't explain it all in a few lines, so if you wish to learn more about your relationships, I would advise you to book a session with a professional astrologer. This type of analysis requires the time of a consultation, and is very intimate since it includes both the birth charts analyses and how they interact together.

Moreover, you should know that in astrology, there is no such thing as "incompatibility." The purpose of a love compatibility analysis is more to reveal the strengths and weaknesses of a relationship, to shine the light on each person's needs, and to determine what works.

Of course, there are astrological placements you can focus on to better understand your relationship to love and sex. First and foremost, you need to look at where Venus and Mars are in your natal chart.

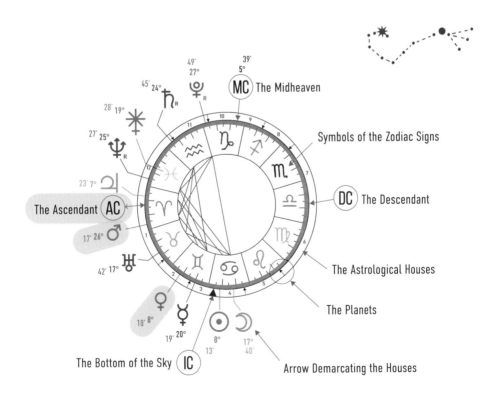

To know which signs are placed in Venus and Mars, you need your birth chart. When I told you in the first chapter that your birth chart was essential, I meant it: it's important for all your placements. On the previous page, I use the example from the birth chart on page 24 to show you where to find your Mars and Venus placements.

Venus and Mars: Your Romantic and Sexual Signature

Venus is what we call a "feminine energy."* This planet will unveil how you deploy your love; she tells you precious information about how you love, your love language, how you enter new relationships, your affective needs, and everything you love in general. It also explains your relationship to beauty and harmony. It's an energy that invites you to embellish your life.

Venus is a passive energy, and through that it represents your ability to be receptive, especially when it comes to financial abundance. That's not all. Venus will also indicate how you receive love during the sexual act. Do you really allow yourself to welcome your partner's love, energy, and tenderness?

Inversely, Mars is what we call a "masculine energy."* He has an active energy that questions combativeness.

Mars is the pulse of life, the action and courage principle. Which means Mars is your boldness, the way you try new things and how you act. This planet explains how you use and profit from

* **Reminder:** we are here talking about the yin and yang polarity, not about gender or sex. The feminine and masculine energies living within us have nothing to do with gender.

the energy of your solar sign. Mars's energy is direct and penetrative, and it needs a purpose and constant motion.

As a symbol of passion and life spark, Mars also symbolizes your sexual needs. The red planet is the placement that reveals how you act during sexual acts, and how you connect to the "masculine" energy yang.

As explained in the first part of the book, that's why it's more relevant to look at the Mars placement when it comes to questions of sexuality in astrology, instead of the Sun placement.

Before we begin our new journey through the stars, I want to specify that these planets have various meanings other than the ones described here. However, we will only focus on their relationship to love and sex. If you wish to know more about the broad energies of Venus and Mars, run to my Instagram account. You can also listen to all the podcast episodes I have dedicated to these planets.

Moreover, I use the pronouns "she" and "he" to discuss the energies of the planets Venus and Mars. I will use these pronouns because they relate to the vibrations the planets emit. But know that these placements apply to you no matter your gender.

All right, if you haven't done it already, I'm inviting you to go grab the screenshot of your birth chart so we can begin our immersion in the energy of the planet Venus, then the energy of the planet Mars.

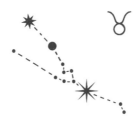

Venus through the signs

Venus in Aries is a go-getter; they have no time to lose. When they have a target, they get into seduction mode, wear their finest assets, and go hunting.

They are passionate, easily fall in love, and love intensely. But the downside is that they can quickly get bored and lose interest. With Venus, everything is fast and strong.

So, if you meet someone with a Venus in Aries, let them seduce you, but don't hesitate to resist a bit. In the end, they enjoy it.

♥ amal's love advice ♥

If you're dating someone with this placement, directly set the bases of the healthy relationship you want to build. Be honest and firm when it comes to your boundaries.

Venus in Taurus

Very comfortable in this sign, Venus loves with a sensual and carnal love, and is here to fully enjoy the pleasures life can provide.

They might need time to be wooed, but once their heart is won over, they can be quite romantic.

Very tactile, Venus in Taurus needs physical contact to feel loved. They also need to be reassured, and to know they can count on their partners.

♥ amal's love advice ♥

If you need to ask someone with this placement on a date, don't skimp on fine things: nice spas, good restaurants . . . pamper them!

Venus in Gemini

Venus likes to flutter around in this casual and mischievous sign. Flirting here, seducing there: their heart sways and their love twirls.

In love, Venus needs to feel an intellectual connection with their partners, for they are sapiosexual: aka, attracted to educated people who can stir them up intellectually.

With their childlike soul, they like to laugh and play. To keep them close, make sure to stay fun and casual, and most important, to stimulate their cerebral side.

♥ amal's love advice ♥

With someone who has this placement, I would advise you to let go. If you tend to plan everything when it comes to love—well, that's not great, because love is a wave that takes you away—let go instead. It will allow you to reconnect to your inner child. You should also focus on communication. If you have something to say, say it!

Venus in Cancer

Soft and sensitive, Venus in Cancer tends to be shy when it comes to love.

They need to feel totally safe, and to be comforted before they can open up. For that reason, they create a nice little nest for themself, where they can share an intimate and deep relationship with their partners.

Venus in Cancer loves tenderly and with sensitivity and feels their emotions intensely.

♥ amal's love advice ♥

For someone with this placement, I'd advise you to make them feel safe with a musical date, or a visit to a museum with a history theme so you can both dive into the past. It will allow you to connect to your emotions safely!

Venus in Leo

Venus in Leo roars with passion and ardor. They love with a strong, powerful, and extravagant love.

Generous and romantic, they never do things halfway, and are ready to seduce you through grand and spectacular gestures. But be careful, they expect you to do the same for them.

If they don't get what they want from you, they might become a little bit capricious. But bonus points for you if you shower them with compliments: Venus in Leo loves that!

♥ amal's love advice ♥

Humor, humor, and even more humor! Try to let go: everyone has a fun side, and it's time to bring it out. Have your partner meet your group of friends, because they will love to discover your friend circle. Moreover, presence makes a Venus in Leo melt. So be yourself, but a bit more like Beyoncé. A little concert, anyone?

Far from being easy to seduce, Venus in Virgo can seem aloof at first glance. Until they are sure that your intentions are pure, they usually won't let anything show. Once they trust you, they will give themself body and soul, and will show you their love by taking care of you and by being always ready to help. Loyal with a big heart, you can always count on them, no matter what. They are also very observant and will take note of everything you say, to then treat you later.

♥ amal's love advice ♥

Create a safe space for Venus in Virgo's emotions, for they need to feel safe to open up to you without concerns. Make them understand that with you, they can be vulnerable without being judged. Don't hesitate to share your dreams and professional goals with them: they love everything related to careers and will support you!

Venus in Libra

Casual and romantic, Venus in Libra loves love, and gives a lot of importance to the relationships in their life. Idealistic, they dream of a relationship just like in the movies, where everything is perfect. They're looking for constant harmony and might try to avoid conflicts at all costs.

Naturally sweet and charming, they can sometimes flirt without even realizing it.

♥ amal's love advice ♥

Show them that relationships aren't perfect and *shouldn't* be perfect. Don't hide your flaws, and make Venus in Libra feel comfortable with their own flaws. Take things lightly, don't judge them, and teach them to let go and to build a relationship step-by-step. And to make them melt, don't hesitate to use a touch of subtle humor!

In this very intense water sign, Venus is magnetic and sensual. They emit a mysterious and seductive aura, but they can seem inscrutable.

They feel everything strongly, so they also protect themself a lot. Their heart isn't easy to access. Don't expect them to tell you they love you first.

When it comes to love, Venus in Scorpio needs an intimate and deep relationship. They want to share everything with their partners.

♥ amal's love advice ♥

Being mysterious is nice and all, but you want to discover the person they are inside. Ask them questions to get to know them. They particularly enjoy complex questions, and hate general, unoriginal ones. Be attentive and make sure you create an emotionally safe space for them.

Venus in Sagittarius

Venus in Sagittarius is adventurous: they like to explore the romantic feeling and are very effusive.

Optimistic, sociable, and friendly, they have big ideals but can struggle to seriously commit, for fear of losing their freedom.

Very independent, they need to know they can have their own space if they decide to date someone.

♥ amal's love advice ♥

If you were planning on calling them every night and texting every hour, give it up right now! However, you can spend very special moments with Venus in Sagittarius. But don't plan dates too ahead of time. It's best to ask them what they want to do on the same day, and to allow the date to flow according to your current whims.

Venus in Capricorn

In this responsible, serious, and calm sign, Venus is first and foremost looking to build something strong with their partners. They value stability and emotional security and need to feel like there is a purpose, a vision.

One thing is sure, you can always count on them, because they are loyal to their values and will never let you down if you need them.

♥ amal's love advice ♥

Take your time, babe! Venus in Capricorn needs to feel like you have a life besides the relationship, so talk to them about your projects and your career. It's really a placement that will never be uninterested in your professional life. On the contrary, they think it's a great way to get to know you. And most importantly, be thoughtful and sincere.

Venus in Aquarius

Open-minded, Venus in Aquarius has a great need for freedom and independence, and most importantly, they need to be intellectually challenged.

When it comes to love, they will flourish in unconventional relationships.

They accept their partners for who they truly are, with their differences and originality.

They also tend to see their partners as friends whom they love in a different way.

♥ amal's love advice ♥

It's said that the three pillars of a couple are friendship, sex, and love. Here, it's important to cultivate the friendship side: going out, nights in, shopping sessions, getting drinks, and catching a last-minute movie will give rhythm to the relationship. So, be friends before lovers.

The ultimate exalted romantic, Venus in Pisces loves with a strong and unconditional love.

They daydream a lot and are idealistic, so much so that they can easily get carried away by their imagination and fantasize in their relationships. And so, they need to learn to be more down-to-earth.

When it comes to love, they need to feel a deep and intense connection, with, if possible, an added spiritual dimension.

They know how to show incomparable compassion and need to be careful not to create a savior/saved dynamic.

♥ amal's love advice ♥

A romantic dinner, a poem, musical references sent by text to let them know you're thinking of them . . . In short, express how you feel and the emotional connection you experience with them. Venus in Pisces shouldn't feel time passing around you, but they should feel like they're in a bubble away from time. For a Venus in Pisces, time stops when they kiss you.

Mars through the signs

Mars in Aries

Mars in Aries is smoking hot and feeling comfortable. Their sexual energy is lively, and they have an impressive libido.

To seduce them, there's no need to beat around the bush: the more direct, the better. And get ready to get physical all night long . . . and then again in the morning. No time off!

Mars in Aries's inner fire is vivacious; they need action and an intense sexual activity.

Mars in Taurus

Unlike the Mars in Aries, Mars in Taurus likes to take their time.

They need security and to feel comfortable with their partners before they can reveal themself fully. But once they trust you, they are tender and sensual.

Soft and endurant, and a bit romantic, they set the mood: their temperature rises slowly but surely, and the sexual act can last for a long time.

Mars in Gemini

Because this pairing is a sapiosexual, it's by using words and sexual communication, as well as possessing great knowledge, that you will seduce a Mars in Gemini.

This placement needs to talk and express their sexual feelings.

Their libido can be quite changing. One day they might be on fire, then completely disinterested the next.

Their adaptable nature makes them flexible to any fantasy, so get ready. And bonus points if you like to talk during sex!

Mars in Cancer

Very soft, Mars in Cancer needs a deep feeling of safety before they can jump in with both feet.

Once they trust you, this placement requires a deep connection with their partner.

To them, sexuality is about two souls connecting, and allowing the existing bonds between people to strengthen. So, to seduce Mars in Cancer, take it slow and tender, and be patient.

Mars in Leo

"Roaring with pleasure": thus is the mantra of this placement.

With a passionate nature, Mars in Leo is smoking hot, with a big libido. But they're also romantic.

With them, expect the sublime, for they like to do things big, whether it's a bath with rose petals in a five-star hotel, or making love on a beach at sunset.

So, here's some advice: try hard to seduce them because it'll never be too much.

Mars in Virgo

Despite the appearance or what they may lead you to believe, Mars in Virgo is hypersexual.

However, to see this side of them, you will have to get them to trust you. But believe me, once they reveal this side of themself, get ready to really enjoy *yourself*.

Mars in Virgo likes to try everything, and because they have an observant nature, they will think about all the details to satisfy your pleasure and theirs.

A bit of a control freak, you'll earn points with Mars in Virgo if you let them take charge . . . if you know what I mean.

Mars in Libra

Very attentive to their partner's sexual needs, Mars in Libra will do everything they can to satisfy their partner first, and they might even put their partner's pleasure first.

The ultimate romantic, they will pay close attention to the little things that make the experience unique and hard to forget: candles, a sexy outfit . . . and it's even better with the sound of rain outside the window.

Mars in Scorpio

Quite spicy, Mars in Scorpio likes sex and isn't afraid to say it. This is probably one of the zodiac's most sexual placements.

To Mars in Scorpio, sex is a space for exploration of the being and its darkest corners, but also a way to purify ourselves—which means they like to try *all* the fantasies. So, get out your sex toys and get ready for an incredible experience.

Keep in mind, however, that they will need to feel a great level of intimacy before they can fully reveal themself to you.

Mars in Sagittarius

Mars in Sagittarius is afraid of nothing. They're very playful and like to explore everything outside of their comfort zone.

Hot, flirtatious, and most importantly, passionate, they will also need to know they can remain independent and free no matter what.

They're not a fan of romance either, so between you and me, keep it fun: the more you keep your relationship casual and positive, the better.

Mars in Capricorn

Prepare yourself because Mars in Capricorn knows how to take the lead.

At work they remain focused on their tasks, which doesn't stop them from being just as applied in bed, and then . . . it can last all night!

Grounded and practical, they're direct and won't beat around the bush. And you can be sure they'll have a well-organized plan to take you to nirvana. Also discreet, Mars in Capricorn will appreciate keeping things private, even sometimes secret, with their partners.

Mars in Aquarius

Very versatile, Mars in Aquarius can be whimsical and paradoxical. Their libido is also quite changing.

In bed they might have a thousand fantasies, and they'll be willing to try out a lot of things. But truth be told, they really need to feel a great bond with their partners.

Mars in Aquarius is the type of placement that might prioritize "friends with benefits" relationships, something without ties and complications. Their motto: *make love, not war!*

Mars in Pisces

Spiritual and connected, Mars in Pisces needs to live deep, intense, and transcendental experiences.

They're romantic in bed, and like to connect body to body (and most importantly, soul to soul) with their partners. To them, sex is a way to connect to the divine within us.

With this spiritual dimension, they can enjoy practicing the tantra, and use their orgasms to reach a higher level of consciousness.

Astrological Compatibilities

AMAL AND I don't have a Moon in Gemini for nothing: we like to play and laugh. When we thought of the idea of a compatibility chart, we looked at each other all starry-eyed and enthusiastic! So here we go: I've made you a compatibility chart!

You get to discover it by looking for your Venus and Mars signs, as well as your partner's signs. This is of course something to take lightly and with a grain of salt. As I've said before, love compatibility in astrology is *muuuuchhh* more complicated than that.

Let's check out the chart!

	Aries	Taurus	Gemini	Cancer	Leo	Virgo
Aries	🚀	👽	✨	⚡	💜	👽
Taurus	👽	🚀	👽	✨	⚡	💜
Gemini	✨	👽	🚀	👽	✨	⚡
Cancer	⚡	✨	👽	🚀	👽	✨
Leo	💜	⚡	✨	👽	🚀	👽
Virgo	👽	💜	⚡	✨	👽	🚀
Libra	🔥	👽	💜	⚡	✨	👽
Scorpio	👽	🔥	👽	💜	⚡	✨
Sagittarius	💜	👽	🔥	👽	💜	⚡
Capricorn	⚡	💜	👽	🔥	👽	💜
Aquarius	✨	⚡	💜	👽	🔥	👽
Pisces	👽	✨	⚡	💜	👽	🔥

Legend:

💘 Wow! Your placements are in the same sign, meaning you have many things in common, and things flow easily between you.

💜 Bingo! Your placements have the same element: they understand each other and move in the same direction, which means that everything seems natural and harmonious between you.

🔥 We love it: your placements are opposites, and you know what they say . . . opposites attract. So yes, some things might be a challenge in your relationship, but it's for the best, and will only help you grow.

✨ Your placements are complementary: they're different but get along well, because they go in the same direction and have ways of working that complete each other.

⚡ There's some friction and tension here. Yes, it can be quite attractive, but be careful: you'll have to work to understand each other, because you function in different ways.

👽 Your placements have nothing in common. They struggle to understand each other, and don't have a lot of common ground. So, to make the relationship move forward, you both need to work and remind yourselves that you're on the same team.

Libra	Scorpio	Sagittarius	Capricorn	Aquarius	Pisces
🔥	👽	💜	⚡	✨	👽
👽	🔥	👽	💜	⚡	✨
💜	👽	🔥	👽	💜	⚡
⚡	💜	👽	🔥	👽	💜
✨	⚡	💜	👽	🔥	👽
👽	✨	⚡	💜	👽	🔥
💘	👽	✨	⚡	💜	👽
👽	💘	👽	✨	⚡	💜
✨	👽	💘	👽	✨	⚡
⚡	✨	👽	💘	👽	✨
💜	⚡	✨	👽	💘	👽
👽	💜	⚡	✨	👽	💘

How Compatibility
Works in Astrology

As I've explained before, to do an actual love compatibility study you need to do a synastry. That being said, I can still give you a few pieces of advice to understand how compatibility works in astrology. And in fact, that's why I created the chart on pages 122–123.

In the first part of this book, I explained that all the signs have an element and a modality. These are the things that can allow us to compare you and your partner to see if the planets are aligned.

The signs are the most compatible when they have the same element. Thus, these signs are very compatible:

- Earth signs: Taurus, Virgo, Capricorn
- Fire signs: Aries, Leo, Sagittarius
- Water signs: Cancer, Scorpio, Pisces
- And finally, air signs: Gemini, Libra, Aquarius

But signs can also be compatible with the signs from their complementary element: air with fire (since air feeds fire), and water with earth (since water nourishes the earth).

Which means that there is a compatibility between:

- Air and fire signs: Gemini, Libra, Aquarius, Aries, Leo, Sagittarius
- And earth and water signs: Taurus, Virgo, Capricorn, Cancer, Scorpio, Pisces

Now you can compare your respective planets according to what I've just explained.

Your Turn Now!

Take your Astro notebook and copy the following chart, then fill it up with your birth chart and the birth chart of someone of your choosing. In each column, write down the signs in which the personal planets are found (Sun, Moon, Mercury, Venus, and Mars) and add each sign's element next to it. If you have Venus in Gemini, for example, just add "air" after Gemini to make it easier for you to analyze the compatibility.

	You	Your hot crush
Sun		
Moon		
Mercury		
Venus		
Mars		

Now that you've filled up the chart, you can have fun comparing your placements to see if you are mainly compatible or not.

Compare your Sun, Moon, Mercury, Venus, and Mars placements, but you should also compare the Sun with Mars, the Moon, Mercury, and Venus, and so on with all the planets.

To help you understand how this works, let me give you a few examples:

- If your Sun is in Sagittarius, and the other person has a Mars in Aquarius: bingo, these sings have complementary elements (fire and air).
- If your Venus is in Virgo, and the other person has a Moon in Capricorn: your yin planets are in signs of the same element.
- Now let's say your Mars is in Aries, and the other person's Mars is in Cancer: at first glance you are less compatible. But you can only determine compatibility by considering the other placements as well, since only then can you have a clear picture.

However, I want to specify that this is a very "simplified" way of knowing whether you are compatible with someone. Again, don't take it at face value; it's in fact much more complex.

And remember that no one is "incompatible." So, if this little exercise leaves you with more questions, or makes things seem complicated, know that nothing and no one can decide for you if you're happy in a relationship or not. It's important to stay in tune with what your soul and heart are telling you.

Giving You the Tea

So, this is the moment for Amal and me to tell you a bit more about us, and what we think of the Venus and Mars placements, according to our own personal experiences. Watch out, it's about to get juicy in here!

☾ Amina

Mars and Venus are both in the Pisces signs, so I love having very deep relationships, with an intense connection. I need to know I can completely open up, and I like to have a partner who is capable of welcoming all my depth and vulnerability.

I also need a spiritual connection, something that transcends this plane of existence: a connection from soul to soul, a feeling of "I don't know why, but I feel like I've known you for ten years even though we just met."

I am heterosexual, and I've always been attracted to men with placements in Scorpio, especially for the Sun, Venus, and Mars signs. I find them irresistible. But I also connect really well with Venus in Taurus, Virgo, Scorpio, Pisces, and Cancer.

I am extremely romantic, even a bit idealistic and a bit of a daydreamer. What I love about astrology is that it allows me to understand this about myself, and thus to take off the "pink" filter I sometimes see over everything so I can reconnect with reality.

☾ Amal

It's my turn! My Mars is in Scorpio, and my Venus is in Libra. I like intense relationships when it comes to connecting to each other, but I must confess that I need time to get to know someone before I can date them. I like to know everything about them first.

My Sun in Virgo knows exactly what I want from a relationship, so I have nonnegotiable conditions that are well in place.

It may not look like it at first glance, but once I'm in love, I can be very romantic, devoted, and attentive.

I like sexual relationships full of charm and passion, but most importantly, I like when they make me feel as if I'm hungover after a party, so I can say, "Wow! That was so insane; my whole body is sore!"

Love and Sex Through the Fifth, Seventh, and Eighth Houses

I HAVE JUST DETAILED the energies of Venus and Mars to help you better understand your relationship to love and sex according to these placements in your birth chart. You can imagine that astrology is a complex field (I've also told you that many times in this book) and so there are other things that can offer us answers about love and sex in a birth chart.

In the first part of this book, I told you about astrological Houses. These Houses represent the different aspects of someone's life, with each House corresponding to a specific aspect.

Each House can be studied according to three criteria:

- The planets present in the relevant House;
- The sign in which the House is;
- The position of the planet that rules the sign of your House (and here we do step in to a more delicate and detailed analysis that is easier to figure out with a more advanced knowledge of astrology).

When it comes to love and sexuality, the fifth, seventh, and eighth Houses are the most relevant ones to explore. You can see where they are placed on the birth chart on the following page.

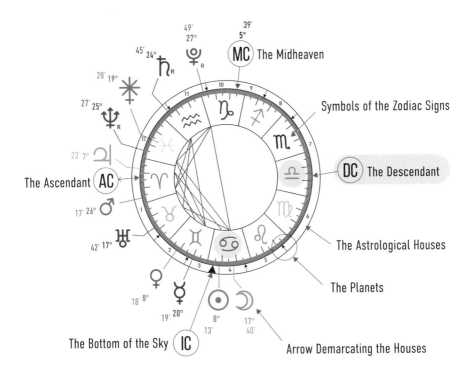

49'
27°

39'
5°

℞ ♇℞

(MC) The Midheaven

45' 24° ♄℞

28' 19° ✳

Symbols of the Zodiac Signs

27' 25° ♆℞

23' 7° ♃

The Ascendant (AC)←

(DC) The Descendant

17' 26° ♂

The Astrological Houses

42' 17° ♅

The Planets

♀

18' 8° ☿

19' 20°

8° ☉   ☽ **17°**
13'   **40'**

Arrow Demarcating the Houses

The Bottom of the Sky (IC)

Before I can give you more details, I want to specify that these Houses have many other values and are tricky to analyze. I will only focus here on their meanings related to love and sex, but if you want to go further, don't hesitate to listen to the episodes of my podcast on Instagram that are dedicated to astrological Houses.

All right, let's go!

The Fifth House

This is the House of flirting, romance, and casual sexuality. It's also the dating House. So, whenever you go on a dating app to meet someone, you enter the fifth House's energy, in which we have fun and laugh. Everything here is fun, casual, and pleasurable.

The Seventh House

This is the long-term relationship and commitment House. In this House, things are serious between your partner and you. In the seventh House, we commit and/or we get married, for better or for worse.

The Eighth House

This is the House of intimacy, deep sexual connection, and intense spiritual paths. In the eighth House, we show our vulnerability, we discover ourselves deeply, and we bond with our partners. Placed after the House of long relationships, the eighth House also explores the sexual life you might develop with your partner after your commitment.

Analyze Your Fifth, Seventh, and Eighth Houses

It's your turn to play, baby astrologer! It's time to dive into your birth chart again and go into your relationship to love and sex in depth. Take your birth chart and let's go!

Find in your birth chart in which signs the three Houses we focus on are placed, as well as the planets. You simply need to see the sign placed in the first arrow of these Houses. Write down this information in your Astro notebook.

You have no planets in these Houses? You're obviously wondering if you'll end up single. Absolutely not! There are only ten planets for twelve Houses. A lot of people don't have any planet in their fifth, seventh, and/or eighth Houses. Don't worry, it doesn't impact your love or sexual life.

If no planet is in these Houses, you can still analyze the three Houses by basing yourself on two other analysis criteria: firstly, the astrological sign in which the House is placed, and secondly, the master of this sign, as well as the House in which it's placed in your birth chart.

For example: if you want to learn more about your seventh House in Libra, and it has no planet, first analyze the placement of your seventh House in Libra. Then you may look at where Venus is, for it's the ruler of Libra. Study this placement in your birth chart to find out more about your House.

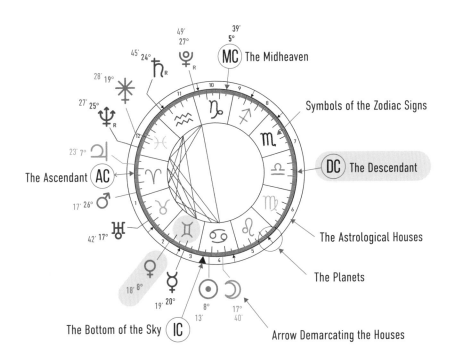

Once you have written down your placements, go back to the first chapter to read the descriptions of the signs' main energies, so you can get used to the vibration.

Now that you have all the info you need, take your Astro note-book and fill the sentences you'll find after the chart with the keywords below.

	Fifth House	Seventh House	Eighth House
Aries	spirited	enterprising	animalistic
Taurus	calm	loyal	sensual
Gemini	casual	stimulating	intellectual
Cancer	soft	reassuring	tender
Leo	passionate	charismatic	vivacious
Virgo	modest	attentive	conservative
Libra	romantic	refined	delicate
Scorpio	intense	deep	transcendent
Sagittarius	expansive	independent	direct
Capricorn	serious	reliable	traditional
Aquarius	ambivalent	atypical	open
Pisces	idealistic	empathetic	spiritual

My relationship to love and romance is

.... *(fifth House's sign)*.

In order for me to get invested in a relationship, I need a/an

.... partner *(seventh House's sign)*.

When it comes to intimate relationships, my relationship to sexuality is

.... *(eighth House's sign)*.

Love Commitment According to the Asteroid Juno

ANOTHER CELESTIAL BODY in your birth chart can tell you more about how you envision love: the asteroid Juno. Below, you'll find the birth chart from page 24, so I can show you where to find it.

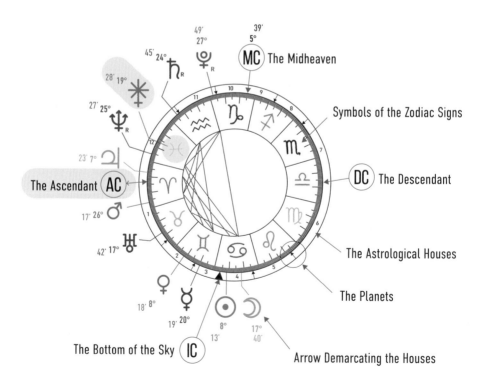

49'
27°

39'
5°

(MC) The Midheaven

45' 24° ♄ R

☿ R

28' 19° ✳

Symbols of the Zodiac Signs

27' 25° ♆ R

23' 7° ♃

The Ascendant (AC)

(DC) The Descendant

17' 26° ♂

42' 17° ♅

The Astrological Houses

The Planets

♀

18' 8°

☿

19' 20°

☉

8°
13'

☽

17'
40'

The Bottom of the Sky (IC)

Arrow Demarcating the Houses

Situated on the asteroid belt between Mars and Jupiter, Juno symbolizes serious commitment in astrology. Thus, it has the same vibe as the seventh House, except that Juno tends to represent the person you will be seriously involved with, as well as your relationship to love commitment.

Juno's sign placement will indicate the qualities someone should possess for you to seriously commit to them.

However, be careful: this information should be taken with a grain of salt. Just because you have a Juno in Capricorn doesn't mean your partners will have this placement, too. I would advise you to look at the inherent qualities of the sign in question. These are the qualities you will unconsciously look for in someone else.

So, taking the example of Juno in Capricorn, you look for serious, stable, and mature partners. You might even feel attracted to people who are older than you. Be that as it may, that person really needs to be ambitious and willing to build a strong relationship with you.

All right, let's go for a little tour of this asteroid through the twelve zodiac signs.

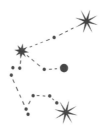

Juno through the signs

Juno in Aries

You need determined and dependable partners. They need to be enterprising and always moving forward, because you want your romantic partners to be dynamic and bold.

Juno in Taurus

You need stable and grounded partners who will help you feel safe in the relationship. You like when your romantic partners are deeply connected to their sensuality and when they like to enjoy the pleasures of life.

Juno in Gemini

You need fun and casual partners who can also intellectually challenge you. You want your romantic partners to be sociable and curious while always being enthusiastic about learning new things.

Juno in Cancer

You need partners who can cover you in softness and affection, and who can be sensitive and considerate. It's important for you that your partners take care of you and the relationship. You also like it when your romantic partners are interested in family and the home.

Juno in Leo

You need charismatic partners that show you how they feel through attentions, especially if they're romantic grand gestures. You like for your romantic partners to be nice, fun, and connected to their inner child.

Juno in Virgo

You need serious, stable, discreet, and organized partners. You prefer for your romantic partners to be aware of the importance of taking care of one's health, and thus the importance of eating healthy.

Juno in Libra

You need charming, sociable partners who know how to compromise. You also like it when your romantic partners are romantic and have an artistic outlook on the world.

Juno in Scorpio

You need intense and magnetic partners who express their passion and are interested in spirituality. You want your romantic partners to be in tune with their sexuality. You also need partners who make you feel unique and make you want to belong to them body and soul.

Juno in Sagittarius

You need adventurous, spontaneous, and enthusiastic partners. You also like it when your romantic partners remain independent and open-minded.

Juno in Capricorn

You need serious and mature partners who are not only responsible, but who also want to build a strong relationship. You also enjoy discreet romantic partners who can show restraint.

Juno in Aquarius

You need free, independent, and original partners who are comfortable with who they really are. You like atypical people, and also need for your romantic partners to be actively involved in a cause.

Juno in Pisces

You need empathetic, sensitive, and perceptive partners who know how to be soft and creative. You like for your romantic partners to be in tune with their spirituality and to help you live in the moment, by letting the flow of life carry you.

We have now finished exploring this third part. I sincerely hope that everything I explained about the placements of Mars, Venus, and Juno, but also about the astrological Houses, helped you feel confident, and that you now have all the necessary knowledge to better understand your relationship to love and sexuality in your birth chart. And now, it's time for fun and . . . spicy things!

4

hot tips

I HOPE THAT you have lived beautiful emotions so far, both power-ful and deep. I hope you've laughed, and that perhaps you've even made this book dog-eared by dint of sharing it around at parties, because everyone was fighting to know more about their birth chart, their match, or their booty call.

We are now at the last part of this book, and as promised it's about to become spicy since I'll be talking about sex toys and sharing hot tips. Hot tips are little naughty pieces of advice I like to give, and which you can explore in your sexual relationships. Indeed, since everything regarding sexuality is taboo in our soci-ety, maybe you need some suggestions given to you by a positive sexuality coach.

In this section I will first tell you more about using sex toys in your sex life; then I will tell you which sex toy I think you should use based on your Sun sign. I've chosen to focus on the Sun sign because it represents your general energy, but don't hesitate to look for your Mars placement, too. For example, if you're a Cancer Sun and a Virgo Mars, you can look at both signs!

Moreover, you can take the time to read my advice for all twelve zodiac signs if you wish to learn more. The most famous toys are presented here, so you can also learn more about hot toys! You might even find some gems to go look for in your favorite sex shop. If you don't know any shop that sells sex toys, or are reluctant to go there, remember that you can also buy these accessories online.

instagram:

- Sanctuarywrld
- Costarastrology
- Moonomens
- Glossy_zodiac
- Nadinejane_astrology

- Ladycazimi
- Drunkastrology
- Alizakelly
- Realastrology
- Bi_astrology

Toys and Accessories: The Good Habits

WHEN CHOOSING WHICH toy to buy, the most important thing is to listen to your intuition, body, and mind. It's essential that you feel no pressure when it comes to sexuality. There is no "good" time to experiment. Only *your* time exists, meaning the moment you will feel the desire to open yourself up and discover this toy or another. And that should only be when you *want* to do it.

Talking Freely About Sex Toys

Be careful: you cannot use sex toys with someone without their explicit consent. It is illegal to surprise someone by putting a sex toy on their private parts, or by penetrating them with it. This is sexual harassment and/or rape and can deeply traumatize your partner.

Before using a sex toy, I invite you to discuss it with your partner to make sure they consent. You should also ask for their consent again before using it during sexual intercourse.

If you have multiple partners, don't mix up the toys. You can use a condom on your sex toys, but it's also very important to clean them with water, right after the sexual act. If you prefer to stay in bed after sex, you can use a wet wipe. In both cases, it's essential that you take the time to thoroughly clean your sex toys with soap and water the next day, as well as rinsing and drying them.

And most importantly: don't leave your toys laying around. Try to find a place to store them, like a little house for your favorite accessories.

how do i bring up sex toys with my partner?

- Tell them you would like to use sex toys and ask them what they think.
- Offer them to take your sex toys out, so they can see what would interest them.
- Reassure them: a lot of people think that if their partners want to use sex toys, it means they aren't sexually satisfied. So, reassuring them is a kind first step that will make them feel good!
- Offer to pick a sex toy together.
- Offer to use the same toy you use to masturbate, if you have one. What matters is for you to explain why you love it, what it stimulates correctly, and why. It could help your partner better understand what turns you on.

Why Use Toys?

Using erotic toys can help you discover more about your sexuality, explore more sensations and feelings, and to experiment. But it doesn't add any spark to a relationship, and it can't save it, either.

In our society, and especially in heterosexual relationships, the woman is often tasked with the duty of spicing up the sexual relationship. This goes hand in hand with the mental burden of always looking "beautiful" and not "letting yourself go" to be desirable to your partner. Women are raised to answer to these injunctions, because society forces them to take the blame when their partner is unfaithful, as if cheating was caused by a "frustration" and thus a woman's inability to "satisfy" her partner. This is a strong social pressure, and I would like to deconstruct all these thoughts by telling you that in every relationship, sexuality is between two partners and sex toys can't "save" a couple who isn't sexually fulfilled.

However, discovering new sensations together, in the context of a healthy relationship, can be fulfilling for both persons. Indeed, sexuality fluctuates throughout a couple's life, and sexual routine isn't inherently bad. It allows people to set boundaries together. And once the bases are healthy, sex toys and new sexual experiences in a couple can bring positivity, but only if both partners want to try.

But once again, if there is a lack of trust, communication, or any other problem in a couple's sexuality, sex toys won't help. They might even make things worse. If you feel like your and your partner's sexual life is facing some challenges, I suggest you:

- See a therapist together.
- Read books on sexuality.
- Express how you feel.
- Reorient your relationship toward intimacy (hugs, showering together).
- Respect your rhythm, and your partner's rhythm.

How Do I Use Sex Toys?

As I've explained earlier, I see sexuality through a scientific lens—thanks to my university courses on clinical sexology—but also through a spiritual and energetic point of view. If you wish to work on your sexual energy, your alignment, and your orgasm on the seven chakras, I suggest you buy manual and glass sex toys to awaken your vagina or your anus, instead of electrical ones that could disconnect you from the progressive sensations that lead to orgasm.

Moreover, here is a question I get a lot: many people wonder if using sex toys might lead to a loss of excitability, and if one becomes less sensitive to manual caresses, whether given by oneself or a partner. So let me say it again: it's impossible for someone to copy the motion of an electrical toy. But if you alternate between manual masturbation (from you and/or your partner) and stimulation with a toy, you won't develop a habituation to the intense sensations the toy offers.

One last thing before discovering the sensorial experiences I suggest according to your placements: sex toys are no exception to the rule I explained earlier about orgasm and how no one "gives" or "receives" an orgasm. Orgasms are taken. So, if you use a sex toy, it's essential for you to want to take this pleasure, and to be open to taking the orgasm.

Another little reminder: when it comes to the intensity of physical sensations, the orgasm is the culminating point of sexual pleasure. Yes, it's quite enjoyable. But once again, it's not mandatory to enjoy a sexual act.

To Each Sign Its Accessory

AND NOW, LET'S discover and play! I hope this chapter will help you in your next sessions of sensory explorations, with or without a partner. To enhance the pleasure in my selections, I didn't only suggest toys but also accessories that can heighten arousal.

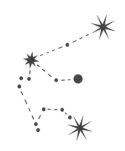

Aries

Why This Toy?

This toy is meant to be used with someone else. Fine, with an original shape, it really reminds me of the Aries's energy.

This toy is meant to be slipped between two people to double the pleasure. Pleasure of the body and pleasure of the toy, it gives more, just like the Aries does with that impulsive energy I find so fun.

It's a bit of a brainteaser to figure out how to place it, but this toy procures a lot of sensations.

I picture it red, because this color is fast, intense, and passionate, which is why red reminds me of the Aries's energy.

Amal's Sex Advice

If you're having sex with an Aries, take this opportunity to teach them slow sex, softness, and the attention one can give to progressive sensations. It could be a good exercise for this placement, who likes to go straight to the point, is very sensitive to adrenaline, and might easily get carried away by a "masculine" sexual energy.

It's time to show them that, sometimes, slowness allows for better sensations, and that doggy style isn't always the best position. (Can we all agree that doggy style has a really Aries energy?) So, let's change position and explore new things for this sign. With this toy, you can make them discover sweet missionary.

Most importantly, don't forget to communicate: if the Aries is impulsive, they can also be too uncomfortable to ask questions about sex. They might even avoid the *after sex debrief.* So don't hesitate to grab them and ask them how they feel. They might panic at first, but at least they'll learn a lot of things!

This toy is perfect for a vagina/penis or vagina/vagina sexual act, but it can be replaced by a prostate stimulator (which is very close to this toy's energy) for other couples.

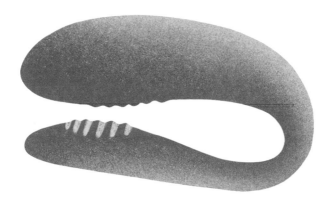

Taurus

Why This Toy?

I didn't pick a purely sexual toy for a good reason.

Just like the Libra, the Taurus represents a certain sensuality. These two zodiac signs are ruled by Venus's energy and have a developed taste for flirting and seducing. And I don't need to tell the Taurus that slowing down is a good thing: they already love to explore the other and play with the sensations. Thus, I associate the Taurus with massage oil.

A massage oil can obviously be seen as a sexual accessory. At this stage of the book, you know that I think sexuality isn't limited to penetration, or purely sexual acts.

And in my view of sexuality, nothing is more sexual and intense than touch, and so putting your hands on someone's body is a way of discovering the deepest sensations. For this placement, I imagine an unctuous massage that awakens the five senses, with the bodies sliding. And this massage can evolve into something else (or not).

Hot Tip

In general, I would advise everyone to add massage oil to their sexual intercourse, even if it's just to massage a body part or to connect to the other person's body.

Massaging your partner's breasts and nipples can be superhot. It allows you to awaken this erogenous zone, and you can also kiss them softly.

Amal's Sex Advice

You have figured it out by now: the Taurus's energy can seduce, flirt, and ground a slow sexuality.

Thus, communication needs to be developed. And communication is the lubricant of interpersonal relationships. For this placement more than for the others, you shouldn't hesitate to practice verbal sex, aka talking about sex before the act, putting words on actions and using dirty talk to step the Taurus out of their comfort zone.

But we know the Taurus, it's not easy for them. So, ask them questions like "What's your fantasy?" or "What do you really want to try?"

And most importantly, don't take it personally if they fall asleep right after the sexual act. We all know the Taurus loves to sleep!

Hot Tip

Suggest a (re)discovery game to your partner. Try a card deck like *Cosmo's Truth or Dare* or *Let's Get Deep* by What Do You Meme?.

Gemini

Why This Toy?

I picked a multifunctional toy for the Gemini. By its shape, it's intriguing, which is one of the Gemini's main qualities, and this toy can be used in many different ways.

This toy is, among other things, a G-spot stimulator. The G-spot is not a myth: it is a zone found a few centimeters away from the vagina's entrance, and it can be stimulated by bending the fingers. There are, of course, sex toys that can do it, and this toy does just that.

Because G-spot stimulation arouses curiosity, hones the interest, and requires practice, I could only imagine this toy for Geminis since they are curious, smart, and love to unveil mysteries. It's thus the perfect toy for them!

I picked the color gray because gray is neutral but quite volatile: it goes with everything, and everything goes with it. And Geminis are very comfortable people who can adapt to someone else or a group very easily. So, a pretty gray toy seemed like a perfect match.

Hot Tip

If your partner has a vagina, don't ask them if they're a "squirter." This expression isn't accurate, since anyone with a vagina can squirt, or have a vaginal ejaculation.

Amal's Sex Advice

The Gemini is a talkative sign who tends to always ask a lot of questions and is always very curious, which is great. I think it's also a sign who is very comfortable with their sexuality: quite grounded, they easily form bonds through sexual relations.

They might just need a little chat to know if the relationship is exclusive or not, so there's no surprise!

Don't hesitate to also explain to them that silence can help someone feel closer to themselves and their partner, and remember to reassure them by specifying that if you're not talking, it's because you're connecting to your pleasure.

Cancer

Why This Toy?

To match the energy of the Cancer, I have picked the bullet vibrator. It's a classic sex toy; one could even say it's vintage. But it reminds me so much of the emotional energy of the Cancer: unimposing, soft, and sweet.

Because this sex toy is relatively small, it can be carried around everywhere. It also offers multiple speeds that can be discovered and used on every part of the body.

In my opinion, it's the best toy for this placement: it's not a very intimidating object, but can be either soft or powerful, depending on the mood.

Hot Tip

If you're looking to try a toy for the first time, I think this one is perfect to start. It will allow you to discover how it feels to add an accessory to your sex life. It's discreet if you wish to keep it to yourself, and has a few different speed options, but it's not the most powerful.

Moreover, know that a lot of erotic stores offer a "first toy" selection, which contains many suitable accessories for people who want to explore new things.

Amal's Sex Advice

If you're having sex with a Cancer placement, don't hesitate to play with feathers on their body, or give them massages (if you want to, of course!). These gestures can light a fire in their tenderness, which might then lead to intercourse.

Everyone can be inspired by the Cancer's energy to learn how to talk about their emotions, and to express themselves genuinely. During sexual intercourse, we feel emotions and pleasure in our abdomen, but also in our entire body. And it's great to share them!

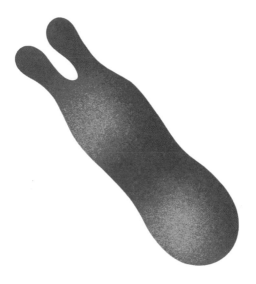

Leo

Why This Toy?

The Leo represents the king of the jungle's energy, which is strong and powerful. For that matter, I really appreciate Leo placements, because these people love seeing their partners' pleasure.

And this toy stimulates both the clitoris and the inside of the vagina. I find it incredible to have a toy that can stimulate two zones at the same time. But it's not for everyone: for very sensitive people, being overstimulated can be unpleasant.

Hot Tip

If your partner likes to be overstimulated, don't hesitate to caress their anus during penetration, for example (after you've asked for their consent). The anus is situated parallel to the clitoris, so when stimulated, pleasure is enhanced!

Amal's Sex Advice

The Leo's energy can be domineering, but during a sexual act, boundaries must be set: the same person won't always be the one leading.

And a little advice: you might have partners who are afraid of losing control. Don't hesitate to talk about it, especially if you're dating a cis heterosexual man. He might need to understand the concepts of virility and toxic masculinity, which terribly affect how we view sex in our society.

Virgo

Why This Toy?

It's widely assumed that the Virgo possesses a wise energy. But in my opinion, they can be both naughty and nice. That's why I have selected a clitoral sucker. It sounds simple, but it's still a quite successful toy. The suction procures a very different sensation than a vibrator.

Everyone knows the vibrator category, which, as its name implies, vibrates on the external clitoris or inside the vagina, against the vaginal lining. The clitoral sucker, however, will suck the clitoris.

During the first try, many talk about a very quick, mechanical orgasm. So, if you want to discover this toy, start slowly, switching between caresses on your clitoris, then the toy, then your fingers, then the toy, etc. . . .

And don't forget that many sex toys offer different settings and intensity levels. Some people forget about that and stick to the same setting. But what's really interesting is trying new things!

Hot Tip

If you have a clitoris and enjoy having sex doggy style, try putting a clitoral sucker on your clitoris (the visible external part of it): guaranteed pleasure!

If doggy style is painful for you, you might have a retroverted uterus. So don't force your body, and instead try doggy style while laying down. In the Kama Sutra, this is called the "Elephant Posture."

Amal's Sex Advice

The Virgo has a strong intellectual energy, like the Gemini. Thus, I advise you to take the time to discuss interesting things, to challenge them with a debate, and to allow them to express themselves: this is what turns them on.

As an earth sign, the Virgo can quickly shut down. And honestly, even if no one likes to get jumped at, the Virgo likes it even less and tends to analyze everything. Slow sex, baby.

Libra

Why This Toy?

I will admit that this conscious toy reminds me of the Libra a lot: it is delicate, sensual, and it's not electrical. The Libra is the sign of sensuality, luxury, elegance, and refinement. In my opinion this sex toy perfectly matches their energy.

The fact that it's made of glass gives it a streamlined elegance, and an enticing design that will appeal to the Libra.

I picked it in pink, because I find it to be both a fun and delicate color, in tune with the energy of this sign.

Hot Tip

I love suggesting glass toys to my community, because they not only allow you to discover yourself even more, but they also eroticize the vagina.

What does "eroticizing the vagina" mean? Let me explain: a lot of people with a vagina can struggle to orgasm through vaginal stimulation. Sometimes it's a question of preference, sometimes it's cerebral.

When the vagina hasn't been eroticized, it won't react to penetration during sexual intercourse. If you only masturbate by stimulating the external clitoris, without ever exploring your vagina with your fingers, or by trying to pleasure yourself with vaginal sex toys, you're unlikely to have a receptive vagina during a penetration. That's why I suggest using these glass sex toys, which allow you to awaken your vagina and stimulate sensations.

Amal's Sex Advice

Don't hesitate to show the Libra that their pleasure is just as important as yours, because this placement craves other people's validation. Make them understand that when it comes to sex, everyone involved should be having a great time. You can even give them a lot of compliments: Libras love compliments, and it's always a pleasure to compliment your partner!

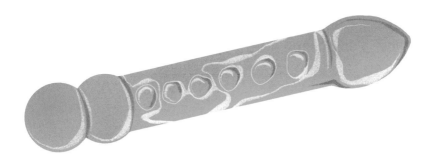

Scorpio

Why This Toy?

The color black, which is intense and deep, always reminds me of the Scorpio.

Black represents mystery, and the Scorpio can have a kinky or even BDSM energy when it comes to dealing with their sexuality. It's a water sign, and yet when it comes to sexuality, I see it as a passionately burning sign.

As with Libra, I picked a glass sex toy, because the Scorpio is going to love teasing their partner at whichever pace they want: they might start slow, speed up, stop . . . and start again. Moreover, this toy has no battery, so the Scorpio can decide the rhythm by trusting their own instinct.

Hot Tip

If you want to try BDSM, make sure to do so under the right conditions, as many movies today fail to reflect the realities of this practice.

In BDSM, consent is key, as are boundaries, safe words to ensure an immediate stop of the act, and many other rules. So, look into it!

Moreover, there are many different levels of BDSM. You can, for example, start with oral sex and a blindfold. This will allow you to forget one of the five senses to enhance the others.

Amal's Sex Advice

Scorpio is my Mars placement. Strange, right? I happen to work in the sexuality field, and I really recognize myself in this placement's description written by Amina. The essential ingredients for me are intensity, passion, and surpassing yourself when it comes to physical contact, to use sexuality as a way to deepen a relationship.

Sagittarius

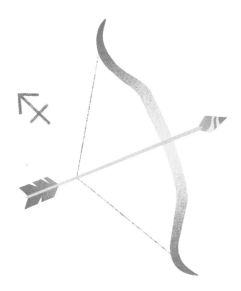

Why This Toy?

For the Sagittarius's energy, I picked an anal toy: it's a way for me to celebrate this sign's taste for exploration.

The Sagittarius possesses an energy that pushes them to discover and seduce like nobody else. They approach things with an open mind and always want to learn more. That's why I believe the Sagittarius can be an excellent sexual partner.

This toy really represents this side of the Sagittarius, which seeks to go further and discover pleasures in sometimes unexplored places.

Hot Tip

As with any other sexual practice, anal sex should be discussed with your partner. Some people will be interested, others won't.

Anal sex requires extra knowledge. You should know that the anal zone is not naturally lubricated. Thus, the top should apply an anal lubricant, silicone based, to make the sexual act more pleasurable.

If you decide to try sodomy with your partner, it's best to use a condom, and not to penetrate the vagina afterward.

Moreover, people often talk about getting an enema before anal sex. An enema should be done with the dedicated tool, an enema bulb. If the penetration is done by a penis or by fingers, an enema is not required, but it is advised.

Amal's Sex Advice

With this zodiac sign, you can allow yourself to be curious. The Sagittarius needs to feel your open-mindedness, and your desire to learn more about their sexuality and yours. So, if you feel comfortable, share everything you're thinking about. And don't hesitate to ask them to try even the craziest things!

Capricorn

Why This Toy?

This toy is a connected egg, and I must say that it reminds me of the Capricorn and their need for control. If you are consenting (obviously), this toy can really work: you just need to insert the egg in the vagina or the anus, and the Capricorn can then control your pleasure!

You must, however, realize that orgasms are very rare with this toy. What matters here is the adrenaline, and the fact that you get to play with your partner, even from afar.

Amal's Sex Advice

The Capricorn also needs to learn how to let go. I would advise you to guide them down that path by suggesting that they slow down their breathing, or lay down and enjoy caresses and kisses to savor the moment and listen to their feelings.

Aquarius

Why This Toy?

When I think about the Aquarius's energy, I think of something unusual, and so I imagine a strange and uncommon shape. Because to allow the Aquarius to connect to the toy, it needs to be as atypical as them.

That's why I have picked a toy you can't find everywhere. It's an accessory that stimulates the inside of the private parts. You can decide to have it fully vibrate or not, and the head can rotate as well, which gives intense sensations.

Amal's Sex Advice

The placement in Aquarius reminds me of excitation, adrenaline, novelty, encounters, and extending sexuality to spirituality.

The Aquarius often likes to discover everything right away and can sometimes get bored. So don't hesitate to ask them what they want to try and why.

And by the way, the "why" is very important when it comes to sexuality, because when we explain to our partner our desires and our sexual practices in detail, the other gets to understand how we feel, and thus learns to know us better. So don't stop at "what do you want?" but also ask "what do you want and why?"

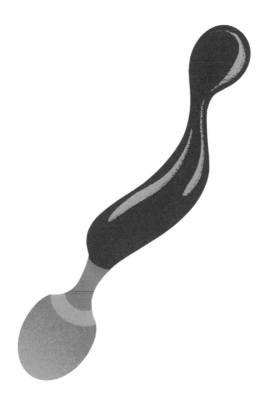

Pisces

Why This Toy?

The Pisces's energy is soft, sensitive, and attentive. So I thought that the perfect sex toy would be these arousing bath salts. Plus, Pisces is a water sign. What better than having a bath with them, to enjoy the perfume diffused by these aphrodisiac bath salts?

Because the Pisces is a delicate sign that notices the little details, a bath will allow them to better discover your respective bodies, and to get physically closer to you and feel you, which they love.

Hot Tip

Everyone should follow the example of the Pisces's sexuality, by being inspired by their ability to connect to their five senses, to try to notice the details, to enjoy the smell, and why not, by taking baths with their partner!

Amal's Sex Advice

The Pisces's energy is very romantic. Pisces love to daydream. Ambiences with rose petals, champagne, and dolce vita are perfect to live a fulfilled sexuality with this zodiac sign.

Conclusion

WE ARE NEARING the end of this beautiful book. What a great journey we've gone on together! We hope that we've helped you explore yourself and your deepest desires through astrology.

Respectively passionate about astrology and sexuality, we have united our strength and vulnerability to give you this book, from our heart to yours, in the hope of helping you radiate and be fulfilled.

Our dearest wish is for you to close this book feeling deeply aligned with yourself: aligned with your heart, your body, and your soul. We hope we managed to guide you into (re)connecting with your superb sexual energy, but also to make you discover astrology which, we sincerely think, is a powerful tool for self-development.

By the way, if you feel like you want to, don't hesitate to explore other practices that could help you feel fulfilled. There are so many: numerology, dance, writing, human design . . . There are so many magical tools one can use to get to know themselves better.

People aren't the only ones with birth charts. Everything that exists on Earth has a natal chart (your cat, your company, your apartment . . .), and given the original French publication date of this book, it is Taurus indeed: sensual, epicurean, and determined . . . And wow, it suits it, right?

In any case, if you loved this book, it's your turn to play: write us on Instagram (@amaltahir and @jaimetroptonsigne) to tell us about how you felt and your journey with our Taurus baby!

Sending you much love and light.

Acknowledgments

THIS IS MY THIRD BOOK, and yet, saying thank you is always a moment that makes me vibrate and feel a deep gratitude.

Thank you to Juliette, our editor at Mango Editions, for accompanying us during this project.

Thank you to my team, for being so invested in my projects, for helping and advising me.

Thank you to my friends and their unfailing support: it's always touching to see how much you believe in me.

Thank you, Amina, for our soft and crazy friendship, and for our baby.

Thank you to my super moon community on Instagram.

Thank you to the Universe and the energy that surrounds me.

And thank you to myself, for always persevering and believing in my dreams.

Amal Tahir
Coach and author
Email: contact@amaltahir.com
Instagram: @amaltahir

Acknowledgments

FOR STARTERS, I would like to thank life and its synchronicity, for allowing me to meet Amal through a session of birth chart reading (which she managed to book, despite there being no slots available), and to thank her for her trust, her love, her kindness, and her loyalty.

I also thank our publishing house and Juliette Magro, for her trust and her precious guidance on this project and more to come!

Thank you to all my loved ones, who supported me during the wonderful journey that was the writing of this book: to my dear and tender Alexandre—my favorite Scorpio in the world; to my sweet friend Elodie—what a Sagittarius you are; and to Samantha: thank you, sister, for being here for me no matter what.

Thank you to my team as well, especially Justine, for all the things you do every day to support the mission of *J'aime trop ton signe*.

Thank you to all my friends. I can't name all of you, but you know who you are.

And of course, thank you to my dear parents, whom I love with all my heart.

Finally, thank you to my community: to all the people who send me love from afar—whether by Instagram DM or email; to my clients for their trust and gratitude; and finally thank you, for reading this book until the end: my endless gratitude.

Amina Sutter
Conscious astrologer
Instagram: @jaimetroptonsigne and @amina_sutter